QUICK GUIDE TO THE 16 PERSONALITY TYPES *AND* TEAMS

Applying Team Essentials to Create Effective Teams

LINDA V. BERENS
LINDA K. ERNST
MELISSA A. SMITH

Published By:
Telos Publications
P.O. Box 4457, Huntington Beach, California 92605-4457
Toll Free 1-866-416-8973 / Fax 1-877-716-8973
http://www.telospublications.com

PRINTED IN THE UNITED STATES OF AMERICA

International Standard Book Number: 0-9743751-3-6

Cover Image: Orange Swirl / ©2001 Damien Jones. Used with permission.
Cover/Layout Design/Illustrations: Kris Kiler Marketing Design.

Acknowledgements
Thank you to

- Our families, friends, students, and clients as we continue to put these powerful theories into practice with teams. They provide us with a never ending laboratory of learning.

- The many people who reviewed these descriptions and gave us honest feedback about what worked and what didn't. We hope we have honored your input. We certainly value it. Thank you.

- And finally, to Jack Gibb, whom we've never met and who is no longer on this earth. In a workshop, he generously shared the four questions teams must answer which we expanded after Liz Post brought them up as a basis for the Working Together workshop conducted by Mike Felts, Liz, and Linda Berens years ago. Thank you, too, to Liz and Mike for getting this work started. The elegant simplicity of Who am I, Who are you? Who are we together? What are we here to do? and How are we going to do it? has served us well in our work with all kinds of teams.

About the Authors

Linda V. Berens, Ph.D.

Linda V. Berens is the founder of Interstrength™ Associates (formerly TRI), which provides organizational consulting and interventions as well as certification of trainers in the Interstrength® Assessments and Method. She has qualified hundreds of professionals to administer and interpret the Myers-Briggs Type Indicator® instrument. Linda is an adjunct faculty member in the Organizational Leadership program at Chapman University and has spent over twenty-five years helping individuals and teams recognize their strengths, transcend their weaknesses, and work together better. Linda is recognized internationally for her theoretical contributions to the field of psychological type and for developing user-friendly training materials for practical application of understanding individual differences.

Linda K. Ernst, M.S.

Linda Ernst is a Senior Faculty Member with Interstrength™ Associates and has extensive preparation in adult learning theory, workshop presentation methods and instructional design. As an instructional design consultant, she has helped organizations develop courses in topics that include leadership development, quality improvement, and communication skills for managers, consulting skills for trainers, and using type dynamics to facilitate teams. Linda is a co-author of *The Guide for Facilitating The Self-Discovery Process®*. Linda is President of Training Resource, an independently owned training and consulting company. Since 1983, she has conducted hundreds of custom designed in-house workshops for a wide range of industrial and organizational clients. She has experience designing and facilitating workshops using the MBTI® instrument for personal development, management development, team building, and for trainers.

Melissa A. Smith, M.B.A.

Melissa Smith is a consultant and trainer specializing in management and organization development. She has designed and delivered numerous skill and management development programs, coached executives to improve group process and personal skills, and assisted organizations in planning and implementing culture changes. A skilled professional development trainer, Melissa is a Senior Faculty Member with Interstrength™ Associates and has extensive experience designing and facilitating workshops using the MBTI® instrument. Her methodology, which is based on action learning principles, is designed uniquely for each client and is tailored for a specific purpose and output. She co-authored *The Guide for Facilitating The Self-Discovery Process®* and is a master trainer of trainers.

Contents

Notepad

Essential Issues of All Teams

Every team has to deal with the same five issues.

- Who am I? Who are you?
- Who are we together?
- What are we here to do?
- How are we going to do it?
- How are we doing? Or how did we do?

Each of these issues is important, yet typically a team jumps right into "Who's going to do what?" and skips the other issues until it gets into trouble and becomes unproductive.

The BLM Syndrome

One of the biggest problems with teams and teamwork is the BLM Syndrome—Be Like Me. We all go around expecting others to be like us and when they are not, we are, at best, surprised and, at worst, angry and full of blame. Looking at personality differences in all aspects of teamwork can help us get out of the BLM trap.

Effective teamwork starts with understanding ourselves and the ways we are different from others. When we know our own value to the team, we are in a better position to value and capitalize on the contributions of those who are different from us. We are also better able to think in terms of the team as a unit, instead of only our own interests—to move from "I" to "we."

How to Use this Book

1. Be certain of your own type through a verification process that includes full narrative descriptions. If an instrument was used to help you assess your best-fit type, be sure you had an opportunity to interact with a professional and to question any instrument results.
2. Read the descriptions of how your type is likely to operate on a team. Realize that you may find yourself not agreeing with parts of the descriptions. Be open to the possibility that they may indeed fit aspects of yourself you are not aware of. They may also not fit because of your uniqueness.
3. Read descriptions of your teammates' types. Don't assume the descriptions will be 100 percent accurate as your teammates are unique too.
4. Complete the worksheets in section 5 to attend to the essential issues of teamwork.

* We owe much gratitude to Dr. Sue A. Cooper for identifying the BLM syndrome and thank her for letting us use this valuable acronym in so many places.

Team and group dynamics are influenced by many factors such as the larger contexts in which the team operates, the organization, the team identity itself, and the mix of individuals within the team.

The Context of the Team

The country and geographic region form a larger culture in which the organization operates. All of these contribute to the economic, political, technical, and cultural climates in which the organization, the team, and the individuals operate.

The Organization

The kind of organization, such as business or non-profit, along with the organizational culture will influence the team functioning just as much as the division of the organization, such as sales, research, operations, and so on.

The Team

Team Identity

Teams have an identity of their own. This identity stems from the interrelationship of the larger culture, the organizational culture, the team configuration, the nature of the work (purpose), and the qualities of the individuals. It is not the sum of the types or preferences or temperaments of the team members.

There are many kinds of teams, including ad hoc, project, executive, management, committee, and so on. Each team has a charter to fulfill a certain role in the organization. Team dynamics are heavily influenced by the nature and purpose of the work to be done by the team.

The Individual

Within this mix of influences are the individual team members, who likely have specific kinds of work to perform and specific roles on the team. Individual members influence the team dynamics as well, so much so that when the composition of the team changes, the team dynamics will change.

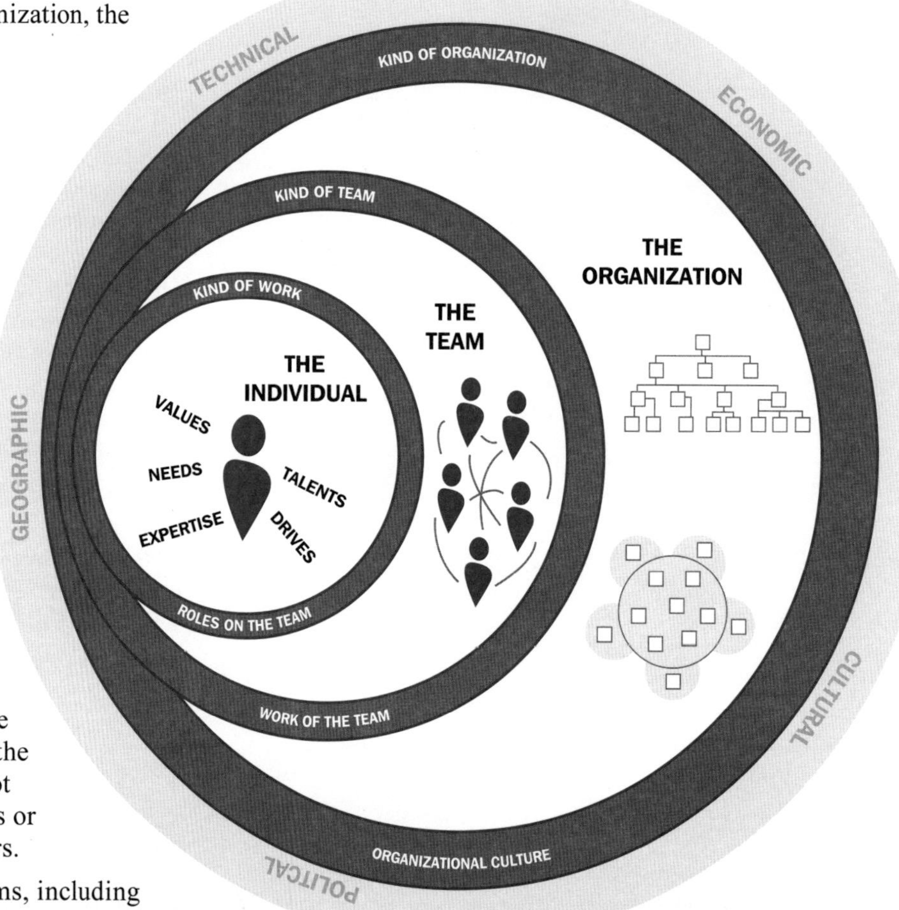

WARNING: An overly stereotypic view of personality type and teams can decrease team functioning instead of enhancing it. As you look at the sixteen personality types and teamwork, keep in mind these interrelated influences on team dynamics. Remember that we are complex and adaptable and our behavior may not reflect our natural preferences but the demands of the situation and the ways we have developed.

The Five Essential Issues

Who Am I? Who Are You?

Team members are individuals first, and each brings different talents, perspectives, values, and experiences to the work of the team. The more self-awareness each team member has, the more actively he or she can contribute. The more each team member knows about the other team members, the better she or he can tap into the talents and experiences of others for better team performance.

In looking at this issue, we start from an understanding that there are sixteen personality type patterns. We describe each of them in terms of a brief snapshot to give a quick overview of the essence of the type as a whole. These snapshot descriptions have been in use since 1989 and have been included in a variety of publications. We also present the typical team-related behaviors in terms of contributions and blind spots.

In this way, we hope to give you tools for understanding yourself as well as understanding your teammates.

Who Are We Together?

This issue involves the key aspects of relationships and communication. Individuals of different personality types are unique in the ways they build relationships and deal with conflict. When we try to forge better relationships, we can easily do something that undermines the relationship instead of improving it if we don't take these differences into account. Personality differences show up in how we tend to communicate as well as how we like to be communicated with. This section of the type descriptions includes keys not only to understanding people who are different from you but to changing your behavior in order to improve your communication and relationships with these people.

What Are We Here to Do?

Amazingly, teams often start right off doing the work rather than clarifying what the work is. Team members assume others see the assignments in the same ways they do. Much conflict and waste of time and resources could be avoided if teams spent a little bit of time to be sure all members share the same view of what they are to be doing and what the outcomes will look like. We briefly suggest the approach to this task that people of different types will take.

Remember to take time at the outset to discuss what the goals, mission, or tasks of the team are (so you all understand). Don't be blindsided by your own BLM agenda. The success of the team depends on getting those agendas out of the way.

How Are We Going to Do It?

Often people treat this as the most important issue on a team. It takes the form of "Who's going to do what by when?" However, this issue involves more than that. It involves both the processes and the production aspects of getting the work of the team done.

People of different personality types will have different preferred approaches to doing the work, but we tend to expect others to do the work the same way we do. This section of the type descriptions includes a look at decision making and responses to change as well since change is a vital part of all processes.

Production is often where our individual talents come to bear the most and where knowing yourself and others can really optimize the performance of the team. And of course, each type's approach to both process and production has pitfalls.

How Are We Doing? Or How Did We Do?

Finally, each team must have some measure of how it is doing. People of different personality types will have different perspectives on what constitutes good and adequate measurement. Don't get stuck in your own preferences here.

Classifying Individual Differences

As we seek to understand individual differences, we tend to gravitate toward classification systems. Having some ways to organize and simply understand the complexities of human behavior is very helpful.

When trying to understand personality, it is important to recognize that all we have to go on is the outer behavior we observe. Much like in the following picture, all we see are shadows.

If we assume what is behind the behavior, we may misunderstand the true nature of that individual's personality. As we can see, we might expect a sphere to have made these shadows, but if the light is right, several other shapes can make the same shape shadow.

So when an organizational setting requires or sets a norm for certain behaviors, individuals of different personality types may exhibit very similar behaviors.

Personality Has Several Aspects

Just as our behavior is not determined by our personality type, the cylinder can have a rectangular shadow or an oval shadow depending how the light is shining.

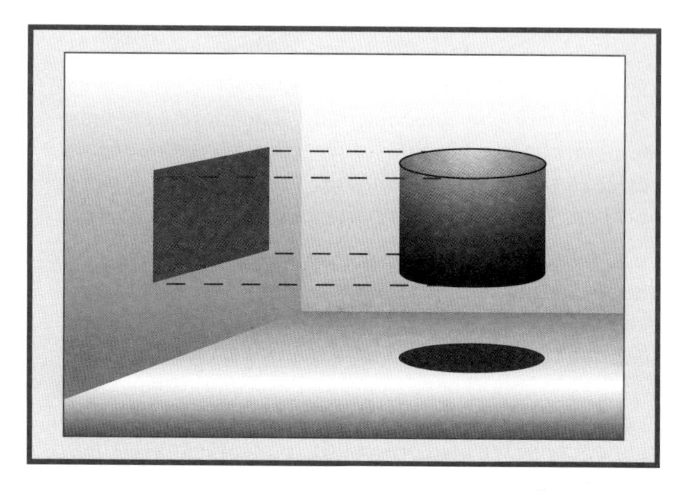

We are complex, adaptable beings, so our personality type can only *predict* ways we might prefer to behave in a given situation. It *does not* determine them.

All behavior occurs in a context—be it work, school, home, socializing, and so on. It is important to understand that our personalities reflect the requirements of these contexts as well as our innate tendencies and how we have adapted to these contexts over time.

The Contextual Self

The contextual self is who we are in any given environment. It is how we behave depending on what the situation requires. The idea of a personality "type" doesn't leave out freedom of action in the moment.

The Developed Self

When the contextual self becomes habitual and ongoing, it becomes a part of your developed self. Personality development is influenced by our choices and decisions as well as by interactions and roles.

The Core Self

This aspect of our personality exists from the beginning of our lives. This aspect of ourselves is in our genes. We are born with a ***tendency*** to behave in certain ways, which influences how we adapt, grow, and develop.

When looking at personality types, all three of these aspects must be considered. Current behavior and adaptations may or may not be consistent with the core self. All are interrelated.

Feeling Sure about Your Best-Fit Type

What Is Best-Fit Type?

Best-fit type refers to the type pattern that fits you best. No one description or pattern will be a perfect match to all of who you are. Your personality is rich and complex, and a "type" or type pattern cannot adequately express all of that richness. Each of the sixteen types comes in a variety of "flavors," and best-fit type means that the themes and preferred processes of that type seem to fit you the best.

Personality Instruments

Sometimes people come to understand who they are through self-reporting on personality instruments. No instruments that rely solely on self-reporting are completely accurate. Ethically, they must all be accompanied by a validation process, preferably involving self-discovery. Many instruments have standards that require face-to-face facilitated feedback with a qualified professional. This booklet is not meant to replace this valuable interactive process but to support it.

Preference versus Measurement

Remember that the results individuals receive from an instrument do not measure an amount of any particular preference but are designed to "indicate" which one they prefer. The score is only a product of the instrument and should not be used as a strength or weakness indicator. A score of 0 for Thinking and 15 for Feeling does not indicate that the respondent does not think! The result merely indicates that the respondent has a preference for Feeling and, if accurate, reflects the accuracy of the indicator for that particular respondent.

No personality instruments that rely solely on self-reporting are completely accurate. Ethically, they must all be accompanied by a validation process, preferably involving self-discovery.

Your Self-Discovery

As you explore the descriptions on the following pages to understand yourself or to understand others, keep the following points in mind:

- If you are using this booklet to find the personality type pattern that fits you best, remember that the descriptions in this booklet describe behavior in the context of organizations, so finding your "best-fit" may be more difficult since you may be having to adapt to various roles inside the organization. If the personality type pattern you thought would fit you doesn't seem to fit, feel free to explore and find one that fits better.

- Workplace environments can provide a powerful context for the expression of the personality. When there is a fit between one's innate tendencies and the organizational context, it becomes a medium for growth and creativity. When there isn't a fit, we can take on all kinds of behaviors as we adapt to the demands of the developing organizational contexts.

- Characteristics presented in the descriptions are key aspects of the personality pattern. This does not necessarily mean other personality types do not have that characteristic. For example, "following through with commitments" in the ESTJ description doesn't mean that other types do not do this, but rather that this quality is central to the ESTJ pattern.

- Don't assume another person will behave exactly as predicted in the descriptions. We are all unique and have various levels of adaptation and development.

The 16 Personality Types*

NOTE: The matrix above organizes the sixteen personality types within "The Temperament Matrix." See *Appendix B: Organizing the 16 Types* for more information.

*Information about each type includes references to the multiple psychological models that are used with the personality type code. These include the Type Preferences, Whole-Type Themes, Temperaments, Interaction Styles, and Cognitive Processes.

Who Am I? Who Are You?

Snapshot

Theme is promoting. Their talents lie in persuading others and expediting to make things happen. They have an engaging, winning style that others are drawn to. Adept at picking up on minimal nonverbal cues, they anticipate the actions and reactions of others and thus win their confidence. They like the excitement and challenge of negotiating, selling, making deals, arbitrating, and in general, achieving the impossible. They thrive on action and the freedom to use all the resources at hand to get the desired outcomes.

On a Team

- Use their talent for negotiating to easily work different sides of an issue before the team, compromising to get things done.
- Tend to be very task oriented. They want to do something, get it done, and move to the next thing. It is often difficult for them to sit still when actions seem stalled.
- Know opportunities don't last so they push for action. They tend to take charge, making things happen. They are pragmatic and expedient.
- Keenly observe team members' nonverbal responses and reactions, instantly seeing what they are up to. They often anticipate the actions and reactions of others.
- Love a challenge, pushing the limits to get the results they want.
- May easily change their position on a team issue as new facts are presented.
- Use their rich store of data to act as consultants.

Potential Blind Spots

- May ignore team members' needs or concerns as they "stay the course" to do what needs doing.
- May be impatient when abstractions don't seem relevant.
- Might bypass authority to focus on expediting.
- Sometimes don't show respect when it is expected because they have keyed into team member motives they don't think deserve respect.

Who Are We Together?

Relationships

How ESTPs Build Relationships

For them, team relationships are about having mutual respect. If they can't respect the other people on the team or the person who commissioned the team, there is no relationship. If they don't respect a teammate, they will dismiss him or her. Trustworthiness in team relationships is also very important so that they can disagree and still be colleagues. Another key to team relationships for them is absolute autonomy and independence. Constraints and limits are seen by them as challenges to work around, but constantly fighting constraints wears on them after a while and such restraints seem to indicate a lack of the respect they insist on. They easily get teammates to follow along—get them to do what they want, communicating a sense of camaraderie. They are comfortable working either together as a team or individually. Although they know feedback is good for them, they usually don't like it.

How ESTPs Deal with Conflict

They often find task-related conflict stimulating and exciting, and they take a direct approach and fight back when need be. Their clear, direct, to-the-point approach may be read the wrong way as they push back to get through the conflict so work can be accomplished. They often get a lot out of conflict and engage their negotiating skills to work through it. They want others to be as direct with them as they are with others. At the same time they want to avoid hurting others' feelings, so they attempt to maintain a respectful and caring attitude, except in a cutthroat environment.

To Forge Better Relationships with ESTPs...

Provide a team environment that allows them autonomy. Avoid directly challenging their authority, but help them see the perspectives of others as factors to be considered before acting. Confront with a consistent and firm approach by giving them direct and to-the-point feedback. Most of all, because recognition or reward runs very high in their value system, give them ways to measure and demonstrate their success

Communication

ESTPs Communicate with...

- Questions to get to the heart of the problem.
- Directives that make things happen.
- A sense of urgency that pushes people to work harder and faster.
- Confidence.
- Confronting, negotiating, and hard bargaining.

To Communicate with ESTPs...

- Give them recognition for their successes and accomplishments.
- Be straightforward and direct, with no attempts at manipulation.
- Show a willingness to negotiate and bargain.
- Provide information about the impact of their actions, rather than abstract explanations.
- Demonstrate a respectful, confident, and positive attitude toward them.

What Are We Here to Do?

They are likely to interpret the job or tasks of the team in terms of the immediate actions to be taken, trusting that they can tactically prioritize along the way. They might resist attempts to spend time for the whole team to get clear on what the goals are.

How Are We Going to Do It?

Processes

How ESTPs Approach Work

They have a tendency to take charge of a situation, especially if no one else is acting and making things happen. They will push the limits to get the results they want. They want to keep their options open; therefore, freedom from rigid role assignments and too many constraints will keep them involved. Otherwise, constraints and limits become challenges to work around rather than guidelines for success.

How ESTPs Make Decisions

They tend to make fast decisions that are realistic and pragmatic. They so rapidly take in the currently available concrete information that others think they take in very little information. They grasp the rich detail from the present information and data they've accumulated and then move quickly to action. They base decisions on what is happening in the immediate, external world that is related to getting the job done.

How ESTPs Respond to Change

Change is all about adapting to the constantly shifting context. Once they see the relevance of a change, they are quick to move to action and implementation. If they don't see the relevance, they will resist and will need some hard facts and perhaps even experiences to show the change is needed.

Production

They tend to be talented at tactical prioritizing, subordinating everything to their priorities as they do what needs to be done. When they see something isn't working, they instantly change their approach. Talented troubleshooters, they are especially good at responding to crisis situations or expediting to take advantage of new opportunities and accomplish tasks quickly.

Potential Pitfalls

- May focus too much on expedience and then become bored or impatient with attempts to slow down to do planning or to consider important strategic or people issues.
- May push the limits too much for the comfort of teammates who don't trust luck and savvy as much as they do.
- Tend to go ahead and produce something without enough background knowledge.

How Are We Doing? How Did We Do?

Since they want a measure of their success, they will likely welcome quantitative evaluations of the outcomes. Spending time revisiting and working through difficult interactions will likely be seen as a waste of time that could be better spent seizing new opportunities.

Who Am I? Who Are You?

Snapshot

Theme is action-driven problem solving. Their talents lie in using frameworks for solving problems. They often excel at operating all kinds of tools and instruments. Keen observers of the environment, they are a storehouse of data and facts relevant to analyzing and solving problems. They thrive on challenging situations and having the freedom to craft clever solutions and do whatever it takes to fix things and make them work. They take pride in their skill and virtuosity, which they seem to effortlessly acquire.

On a Team

- Can excel at helping the team with problem solving, finding an approach or technique to deal with a difficult situation.
- Use all the resources at hand, continually reworking, tweaking, and bringing in new information.
- Tend to be naturally curious and want to understand a situation yet don't accept a theory or explanation as the "truth."
- Want to accomplish—make a contribution; they know every challenge has a solution.
- Operate in an egalitarian, pragmatic, expedient, directive manner.
- Do whatever is necessary to get the job done.
- Delight in accomplishment, often looking easy-going and laid back yet ready to spring into action at just the right time.

Potential Blind Spots

- Tend to enjoy personal achievement more than group or team accomplishments and so may let diplomacy and the "social stuff" lag.
- Might miss implications of their actions.
- May become sarcastic and ignore authority to remain autonomous.
- Often have a hard time agreeing that other people look at situations completely differently.

Who Are We Together?

Relationships

How ISTPs Build Relationships

For them, team relationships are about taking action to solve problems. They tend to focus more on the task to be completed than on the team members doing the work. Relationships often evolve in the process of problem solving. They show they care by solving problems for other team members and are not as likely to express feelings verbally as they are to demonstrate them by doing things with those they care about. They enjoy keeping things simple and showing their teammates techniques and shortcuts that work. They don't like to be on a team when they don't know anyone. Establishing relationships within the team can take a lot of energy for them, so once it's done they prefer not to change it. If they don't feel trapped, they can be very loyal to the team and its members.

How ISTPs Deal with Conflict

Conflict that is centered on how to do things is comfortable for them, but they hate conflict that is heavily laden with emotion. They tend to withdraw so they can sort it all out before they come back and face these emotional situations. Once they have sorted it out, they want to approach the conflict as if it is a problem to be solved.

To Forge Better Relationships with ISTPs...

Provide a team environment that allows for autonomy and individual contributions. They need to be independent, to do things on their own or to be free to not do them. When they resist direction from the team, it is because they want to do things the way they've figured out is the best way. If they feel trapped or coerced, they are likely to resort to independent action rather than team action. They like to choose the timing for when it's appropriate to say or do something. Give them opportunities to solve specific, concrete problems, especially where there is potential for hands-on contributions. Help them check their impulses against the long-range plan. Most of all, avoid direct confrontation; it may result in their insistence on what they think is appropriate and what they want.

Communication

ISTPs Communicate with...

- Listening and questioning that help them analyze a situation and make a plan of action.
- Tips, tools, techniques, and shortcuts for getting something done effectively and efficiently.
- Ways to keep things simple.
- The facts of a situation and what needs to be done next.
- Wisecracks and pithy comments when things get bogged down.

To Communicate with ISTPs...

- Provide the Theorist™e for whatever you are communicating to them.
- Offer specifics about what actions can be taken and the likely results of that action.
- Give them opportunities to solve a problem.
- Specify the outcomes you are trying to achieve and the parameters they have to work with.
- Be straightforward and to the point.

What Are We Here to Do?

They will be likely to interpret the job or tasks of the team in terms of immediate problems to be solved. They will want just enough discussion to make sure they have a good plan of action.

How Are We Going to Do It?

Processes

How ISTPs Approach Doing Work

They want to be independent and to have the freedom to act on their hunches and intuitions, adapt to the situation, and work around whatever obstacles appear. They tend to be curious and will ask questions and try to understand a situation, often taking things apart to figure out how they work. Then they quickly grasp the most expedient solution and take a just-do-it attitude. They don't want to be limited by defined roles but want to have some idea of what is expected of them so they have at least a plan of action going into a situation. A lot of processing of issues will be seen as a waste of time.

How ISTPs Make Decisions

They tend to decide quickly when responding to an immediate need but slowly when they don't see options for action. They're constantly observing, taking in a lot of concrete information, and looking for all the angles. They like to see if the facts fit together, try something, and see what happens. They tend not to document their process, and the systems they develop fit the particular context and may not be transferable to other contexts.

How ISTPs Respond to Change

Once they've figured things out, they may resist changing them, but when the situation demands something other than what they figured out, they quickly look at it from all the angles and then turn on a dime to adapt to what is going on. Talking about change may meet with resistance, but when the situation requires it, they're usually on board.

Production

They tend to have a talent for tactical problem solving and troubleshooting, easily figuring out what tools to use and the best approach to take to accomplish something. They will want to take an analytical and observational approach, quickly scanning the environment for inconsistencies, changes, and new information, and then match the problem to a practical framework for solving problems. Once they've figured out the immediate next step, they want to move on it, see what happens, then move on to the next challenge.

Potential Pitfalls

- May approach a task as a personal challenge and unwittingly increase the difficulty.
- May spend too much time tinkering and may have difficulty seeing the reason for some longer term strategies or somewhat "esoteric" factors to be considered.
- Dislike having to rework something and may resist doing things if they see a "flaw" in the plan that almost certainly will result in rework.

How Are We Doing? How Did We Do?

Since they are constantly analyzing, they will enjoy a brief after-action review that focuses on what worked and what didn't as long as it doesn't get mired in too much interpersonal conflict, which they would rather avoid.

Temperament: **Improviser™** • Interaction Style: **Get-Things-Going™** • Cognitive Processes: **Se, Fi, Te, Ni** | **Si, Fe, Ti, Ne**

Who Am I? Who Are You?

Snapshot

Theme is performance. They are warm, charming, and witty. They want to impact and help others, to evoke their enjoyment, and to stimulate them to act. They want to make a difference and do something meaningful. Often masterful at showmanship, entertaining, motivating, and presenting, they thrive on social interaction, joyful living, and the challenge of the unknown. They like helping people get what they want and need, facilitating them to get results.

On a Team

- Often excel at getting people to open up and cooperate with them. They like helping people get what they want and need.
- Tend to be easy to get along with. They can be counted on to get people to work together.
- Respond to teammates with their genuine caring, generosity, and willingness to help.
- Tend to be easy-going and adaptable yet pragmatic and expedient—doing whatever is necessary to get the job done with efficiency and speed.
- Likely to get the process going and summarize decisions as they occur.
- Get others interested, enthused, involved, and energized around a project, often by using their talent for displaying and presenting information.
- Are great at pulling off "impossible" situations, especially if there is a last-minute crisis.

Potential Blind Spots

- May misread teammates' non-verbal cues and place meaning on them that was not intended, personalizing events and feeling taken advantage of.
- Tend to be uninterested in abstractions unless they are obviously relevant and become frustrated when teammates delve deeper or methodically go from A to Z on a project.
- May not address interpersonal problems to avoid negativity.
- Might not implement or follow an approach suggested by someone else if they don't see it as the best approach.

Who Are We Together?

Relationships

How ESFPs Build Relationships

For them, team relationships are about caring, sharing the work, and having fun together. Warm and friendly, they help by listening to what teammates are trying to do, questioning to get a clear picture, and reflecting back to them what they hear being said. They work very hard to see other people's points of view, although they often want what they want when they want it. They will make the effort to get really involved in the team. They don't want to be left out or have others left out yet often wind up being the center of attention. They are likely to be great tension breakers on the team: whenever they find a situation getting heavy, they say something light to make everyone laugh again.

How ESFPs Deal with Conflict

If they had their way, there would be no conflict. But when there is they usually try to make light of a situation to shift the attention to something more positive. When the team has a problem, they expect real progress to be made toward a solution. If they see no progress, they will likely disengage and perhaps even leave the team if they can.

To Forge Better Relationships with ESFPs...

Provide a team environment that allows them autonomy and freedom from routine and hierarchy. They handle structure but for only a short time—even if they put it on themselves. They like clear direction with freedom to do what they see is needed. Freedom from boredom gives them the strength to do what they need to but don't want to. Don't tell them they "can't" do something. Describe potential roadblocks and problems as challenges. Keep them happy on the team by asking them to do something only once; they dislike the repetition that often occurs on teams. They want to be of value on the team and want an equal exchange. Gain their respect by doing a good job. Most of all provide choices, opportunities, flexibility, and a chance to work with people.

Communication

ESFPs Communicate with...

- Enthusiasm and excitement to help open people up to possibilities.
- Ways to see roadblocks as challenges.
- Presenting and displaying information with a sense of style to get people interested, excited, and involved.
- Drama and stories to get people involved and to stimulate action.
- A sense of fun involvement and lightening tense moments.

To Communicate with ESFPs...

- Offer specific information about what is relevant to the situation so they can focus on the goal and thus filter out the irrelevant from among the swirl of information that comes to them.
- Give them freedom to go ahead and get going.
- Show a willingness to explore what else to try.
- Be honest and genuine with specifics about what you like, don't like, want, and don't want and how they can help.
- Demonstrate energy and optimism in the way messages are communicated, keeping things upbeat.

What Are We Here to Do?

They are likely to first interpret the job or task of the team in terms of what can be done right away. They bring a wealth of information about the practical realities of the current situation to defining the task. Getting everyone on board will be important enough to them that they will be willing to spend some time to help reach a shared vision of the work of the team.

How Are We Going to Do It?

Processes

How ESFPs Approach Doing Work

They are most likely to be stimulating action, getting things going to get things done. They tend to be very good at multitasking and they like it. They have a sort of everybody-pitch-in attitude that engenders team spirit and high energy. When problems occur, they'll want to solve them right away and won't accept "It can't be done" as a solution.

How ESFPs Make Decisions

Decisions usually come quickly for them about what action to take, but they may vary the decision when new options for action are seen. In the time it takes others to notice something, they're already acting on it. They take in a lot of rich detail, noticing minimal non-verbal cues. Usually, this detail is not reported on, just acted on as they adjust their behavior to meet the needs of the immediate situation.

How ESFPs Respond to Change

They are generally adaptable and accept the realities of a situation. They are especially tuned in to people and their reactions. They adapt to change based on what is important in relation to what is happening in their immediate external world, attending to what will make people satisfied and seeking to help them. They can get locked into the ways they've done things when those ways are working and they don't see the relevance of a change. However, they will change when they see how something isn't working correctly and what will work instead.

Production

They provide a keen sense of reality, so they are able to spot trouble early. Often, they are at their best when responding to a crisis and then can move quickly. They like having a variety of projects going at once and, given the tools, often excel at managing those projects.

Potential Pitfalls

- Can sometimes create such a whirlwind of activity that it overwhelms teammates.
- Tend to be much more interested in doing something than describing the process so it can be replicated.
- Tend to take a casual approach to meetings or presentations, which may look random and scattered even when they are well prepared.

How Are We Doing? How Did We Do?

While not opposed to measurement, they are likely to find constant checking in takes up time that is better spent on solving problems. They would prefer evaluation methods to be quick, efficient, and above all, relevant.

Who Am I? Who Are You?

Snapshot

Theme is composing, using whatever is at hand to get a harmonious, aesthetic result. Their talents lie in combining, varying, and improvising, frequently in the arts but also in business and elsewhere. With their senses keenly tuned in, they become totally absorbed in the action of the moment, finding just what fits the situation or the composition. They thrive on having the freedom to vary what they do until they get just the right effect. They take action to help others and demonstrate values and are kind and sensitive to the suffering of others.

On a Team

- Take a resourceful and creative approach to teamwork, with a unique gift of compromising to get quality results.
- Can be great at getting teammates working together toward an outcome, often tapping into what is extremely important to others and to themselves.
- Bring a talent for creatively solving immediate and concrete team problems and enjoy helping teammates solve problems.
- Usually will make something happen when the team is in a crunch to make it right. They are pragmatic and expedient.
- Likely to carry through with their commitments over the long run and are hardworking—often prepared with collected data.
- Approach problem solving by listening to ideas, getting support, and persuading others.
- Tend to judge teammates based on their actions, and if others are good to them, they're good in return.

Potential Blind Spots

- Might ignore systems, policies, and procedures to achieve whatever needs to be done.
- May become quiet when angry, which can lead to withdrawal from the team.
- Can lose track of time when absorbed in a creative moment.
- With their unassuming style, are often blind to their own contributions and needlessly get down on themselves.

Who Are We Together?

Relationships

How ISFPs Build Relationships

For them, team relationships are about having camaraderie, having fun interacting, and solving problems. They value the ability to say anything or say nothing and not have to think about or check what they're doing to get another's approval. They need the freedom to be able to change their mind or direction. They often feel the challenge to balance freedom and their need for privacy with connection. They will do what they can to accommodate other team members, but the feeling of being trapped may suddenly occur. For them, establishing relationships is not about self-disclosing but about helping solve problems. They can get discouraged when a teammate does nothing with the help they offer. They enjoy the give and take and a little bit of competition that occurs in a team. However, when it becomes abrasive and people personally attack others, they become concerned and may attack on their behalf.

How ISFPs Deal with Conflict

Conflict is something they tend to ignore for a while and then work to resolve. When strong values are crossed or when the conflict seems to go on and get in the way of the work of the team, they may withdraw from the relationship. They prefer to focus on getting the work done rather than too much analysis of interpersonal issues.

To Forge Better Relationships with ISFPs...

Provide a team environment with lots of opportunities, choices, and flexibility and a few familiar and friendly people. They want to be doing something that uses their skills and abilities, gives them variety, is stimulating, and lets them have a mission with people. Present a positive, harmonious team climate. Recognize and compliment them soon after an accomplishment. Most of all, let them have their own personal style so they are not boxed in and are free to be what is needed in the moment.

Communication

ISFPs Communicate with...

- Ideas, suggestions for creatively effective ways to solve problems, often quietly and unassumingly made.
- Information for people to use to decide what they want to do, using stories and examples to make their point.
- Listening to what others want.
- Stating what is extremely important.
- Gentle persuasion to get the job done, more often by giving information to prompt action than by giving directives.

To Communicate with ISFPs...

- Give them freedom to choose the information they act on and freedom from pressures regarding expectations—give them the parameters and leave them to their own devices and they will exceed your expectations.
- Provide privacy.
- Offer tangible specifics that show how something will contribute to the desired result.
- Give them time to scan information, tinker with suggestions, and get absorbed in a creative moment.
- Be straightforward, direct, and to the point, avoiding innuendo.

What Are We Here To Do?

They are likely to interpret the job or tasks of the team in terms of the immediate problems to be solved. Given time to scan for more information, they will zero in on what is important and how to take advantage of opportunities while sticking to those important issues.

How Are We Going to Do It?

Processes

How ISFPs Approach Doing Work

They want the freedom to take advantage of all opportunities as they come up, even anticipating future opportunities. They won't want to spend a lot of time hashing and rehashing issues but want to get to the production, working issues as they go. They tend to find opportunities to build relationships and attract loyalties.

How ISFPs Make Decisions

Decision making for them is a process of constantly checking against their values and adjusting their actions as situations change to keep true to what is important. This is not about changing their mind but adapting to situations in such a way as to stay in line with what was important. In this way, they are ready to make quick decisions, but they have given a lot of thought ahead of time about what is important. They base their actions on what is happening in the immediate situation that is relevant to those decisions and also to what will make things better. They get a strong sense of what is needed and what will get the best result and then try various approaches until that result is achieved.

How ISFPs Respond to Change

They are likely to resist any change that disrupts their freedom to adapt to the needs of the moment or significantly varies from the way they've become accustomed to doing things. They can also get locked into the vision of how something is going to be, especially when the envisioned actions are in alignment with what is important. They will embrace a change if it can be shown to be needed in light of the current situation. Just give them solid information and some time to reflect to integrate all of the information.

Production

They tend to be talented at creatively solving immediate and concrete problems. They continually scan the available resources to find just the right idea, color, action, line, word, and so on to pull together a cohesive whole. Once they get going on a project, they like to stick to it, working with it until it feels right.

Potential Pitfalls

- Can be somewhat vague about what they are thinking when they feel pinned down.
- Tend to want to have a lot of variety, which can mean things fall through the cracks unless they have good project management tools or assistance.
- Can be dogmatic in holding onto something they see as important and ignore likely implications and consequences.

How Are We Doing? How Did We Do?

Since they are constantly evaluating, they might not see the need for a formal final evaluation. They just know if they got the right results.

ESTJ Implementor Supervisor™

Temperament: **Stabilizer™** • Interaction Style: **In-Charge™** • Cognitive Processes: **Te, Si, Ne, Fi** | Ti, Se, Ni, Fe

Who Am I? Who Are You?

Snapshot

Theme is supervising, with an eye to the traditions and regulations of the group. They are responsible, hardworking, efficient, and interested in ensuring that standards are met, resources conserved, and consequences delivered. Their talents lie in bringing order, structure, and completion. They want to keep order so the organization, group, family, or culture will be preserved. They thrive on organizing and following through with commitments and teaching others how to be successful.

On a Team

- Likely to establish procedures and activities that provide team members with direction and a sense of belonging.
- Take pride in being accountable; they are committed and responsible to the task. They can be steady, dependable, and predictable team members.
- Can be cooperative team players who have an industrious work-hard attitude.
- Make sure things run smoothly by defining purposes and issues, planning, and attending to logistics.
- Lead in areas that require a responsible, results-oriented approach. They like to have a plan and to follow the plan.
- Likely to expect others to follow rules and procedures, since it fosters the efficiency they so strongly value.
- Relate to others in a direct manner, encouraging cooperative teamwork and motivating for quality performance.

Potential Blind Spots

- May be too quick to tell others what they should or should not do.
- May get bogged down by ambiguous situations. Their focus on concrete data and specific details may make it difficult for them to see the broader perspectives and subtle implications of a proposed action or decision.
- May trigger others to feel put down by their detailed instructions and strong need for control.
- Often are so sure of what to do they may expect others to be more like them—to make decisions the way they would and to have the same opinions of right or wrong, good or bad.

Who Are We Together?

Relationships

How ESTJs Build Relationships

For them, team relationships are about showing caring and concern by providing structure and organization. They enjoy being with people, keeping track of everyone, and staying connected. They want to establish a solid foundation of structure and routine. They often take responsibility for teaching people how to be responsible and what's important so the team will be successful. They tend to have high expectations, of themselves and of others, and tend to push and educate colleagues on the right way to do things. They relate by taking care of what needs to be taken care of, working very hard, and giving of their time.

How ESTJs Deal with Conflict

Conflict often comes when others don't share the load or follow through. When conflict occurs, their concern will be for the maintenance of the group. In interpersonal conflict, they are likely to take a direct approach, facing the conflict head-on and pushing back on issues they feel right about. And they want to be treated in the same way.

To Forge Better Relationships with ESTJs...

Provide a team environment that is stable and that honors time-tested practices and procedures. They enjoy a team approach where no one individual attempts to outshine or draw more attention to himself or herself than the group as a whole. Give them specific examples and comparisons to ground theories and abstractions in practical reality. For them, the team needs to have a time and task focus, agendas, and clearly defined outcomes, and the work of the team needs to follow the agreed-upon plan.

Communication

ESTJs Communicate with...

- Directives about getting to the task.
- Specifics about what needs to be done and by whom.
- Concrete, detailed information, with logical explanations that make sense.
- The rules, guidelines, or procedures to be followed.
- A sense of urgency to get tasks finished.

To Communicate with ESTJs...

- Give them lots of organized information, especially when something new is being considered.
- Present organized, factual information, preferably in writing, early in the decision-making process.
- Offer suggestions about how all of the data connects to the experiences they have already had.
- Provide rules that need to be followed in order for the project to be accomplished in a timely manner.
- Use a confident manner than assures accountability.

What Are We Here to Do?

They are likely to define the job or task in terms of the best way to get it done quickly and what standard operating principles are applicable. They are likely to think that a shared vision of the work of the team comes from the directives provided rather than from a participative process.

How Are We Going to Do It?

Processes

How ESTJs Approach Doing Work

They are likely to first want to be sure they are properly educated so they can be informed and learn the best way to do the job, and they will want this education to come quickly. They also want a clear sense of direction and chain of command. It is critical to them that things feel under control, and when there doesn't seem to be any team leadership, they are likely to take control of the situation.

How ESTJs Make Decisions

While decisions are usually made quickly as to the right step to take now, they may still be more open to other ideas than their brusque manner might communicate. Decisions are usually based on criteria for keeping order and completing tasks and the responsible thing to do.

How ESTJs Respond to Change

When a change is needed or is happening, they are likely to look first to what has been done before, what is tried and true. In the area of something new, they like having some conventional examples to follow. They compare new information quickly to their large internal data bank of life experiences as well as the external rules and standards to be followed.

Production

They tend to be talented at bringing order to chaotic situations by setting up routines, schedules, and standard operating procedures. They quickly see the right way to do tasks and then focus on directing others to do them or jump in and do them themselves. They focus on planning and making sure everything runs smoothly. They are usually driven to make sure tasks are completed on time, and preferably a little early. And while they're at it, they will strive to finish under budget as well.

Potential Pitfalls

- With their trust in authority and designated roles, are sometimes blind to informal leadership.
- Being so accomplishment focused, are often impatient with emerging processes and don't trust that something of value will come from them.
- Tend to focus too much on logistical implementation, neglecting broader strategic and diplomatic issues.

How Are We Doing? How Did We Do?

Accountability and responsibility are very high on their list of items to make sure are in place, so they will want checks and balances and measures of performance so everyone is fairly held accountable.

Temperament: **Stabilizer™** • Interaction Style: **Chart-the-Course™** • Cognitive Processes: **Si, Te, Fi, Ne** | Se, Ti, Fe, Ni

Who Am I? Who Are You?

Snapshot

Theme is planning and monitoring, ensuring predictable quality. Thorough, systematic, and careful, they see discrepancies, omissions, and pitfalls. Their talents lie in administrating and regulating. Dependable, realistic, and sensible, they want to conserve the resources of the organization, group, family, or culture and persevere toward that goal. They thrive on planning ahead and being prepared. They like helping others through their roles as parent, supervisor, teammate, and community volunteer.

On a Team

- Can be highly organized, focusing on completing details of a task and meeting objectives in a no-nonsense way.
- Tend to be orderly, systematic and careful. They work with a steady energy to follow through on commitments.
- Feel responsible for others in the group and often find ways to integrate the varied viewpoints of team members.
- Respect hierarchy and organizational structure and expect others to follow rules and procedures without question.
- Will direct their energy toward providing stability and preserving the team and the organization.
- Tend to inspect work, thoroughly comparing outcomes to a standard to ensure that nothing has been missed and that results are as planned.
- Likely to be dependable, loyal, and dedicated workers who maintain schedules and routines and expect others to do the same, presenting an environment of teamwork (even if one does not exist).

Potential Blind Spots

- May focus on their responsibilities to the neglect of personal relationships and are sometimes seen as too serious and task focused.
- May be overly cautious, especially when roles are unclear.
- Tend to see issues as black or white and make quiet right/wrong or good/bad judgments too quickly.
- Typically frustrated by ambiguous situations, which may keep them from meeting goals.

Who Are We Together?

Relationships

How ISTJs Build Relationships

For them, team relationships are about responsibility and follow-through. They enjoy giving their time and experience and want to set an example of a good worker for associates. They often have a natural feeling of loyalty to their roles and take themselves very seriously, sometimes tolerating conditions most people would avoid. Thoughtfulness and steadiness are the cornerstones of their relationships. They are very private people who don't like a lot of attention. They tend to be observers in a group and will withdraw or stand back rather than press their point if not readily understood.

How ISTJs Deal with Conflict

They tend to put up with conflict rather than confront it—often to the point of personal stress. To deal with conflict they first move away from it, often physically, then they may come back to make the situation better with a calmer focus. They appreciate having conflict managed in a calm, thought-through manner.

To Forge Better Relationships with ISTJs...

Provide a team environment that honors their need for solitude and periods of time for learning, reflection, and planning. For them, change requires time to sit back, take it all in, and think about it—a process that will require patience on the part of teammates. To help that process, be certain to present change in terms of usefulness or practicality. Acknowledge their attention to duty and exceptional use of quantitative and standardizing skills. Make incentives tangible, tried, and proven. On a team, they usually welcome opportunities to develop their interpersonal communication skills and will appreciate anyone who "gets" their subtle sense of humor.

Communication

ISTJs Communicate with...

- Questions about what happened before, what is needed/expected now.
- Information about prior experiences.
- Concerns about how well something will work or not work in the future.
- Practical realities about what's been tried and how that worked.
- Steps and sequences of what should happen to get something done.

To Communicate with ISTJs...

- Give them the specific, concrete facts of a situation.
- Provide lots of practical, factual, and written information early on so that they can check it against their vast internal data bank.
- Give them time to reflect, analyze, research, and plan.
- Be prepared with your own data and plans.
- Give standardized, scheduled, and consistent feedback that includes examples.

What Are We Here to Do?

They are likely to listen, observe, and clarify what is expected. Once that is clear in their minds, they will tend to interpret the job in terms of the logistical plan needed to carry it out, focusing on the pieces of the project and how they fit together.

How Are We Going to Do It?

Processes

How ISTJs Approach Doing Work

They will focus first on getting an orderly and systematic plan in place. They want roles clearly assigned, recognizing the importance of clear lines of authority with clear expectations. They are likely to feel responsible for the work of the whole team and may wind up overworked. Being prepared and able to follow through is very important to them.

How ISTJs Make Decisions

They tend to decide quickly when they believe they understand the situation and the desired outcome. The decisions that come easily for them are ones about the logistics of a situation, so their focus will go to those kinds of situations. When more complex strategic decisions are needed, they may feel overwhelmed and exhausted or impatient. When decisions related to members of the team are called for, they tend to be as helpful as possible.

How ISTJs Respond to Change

They face change cautiously. When the situation is unfamiliar, they first try to relate it to their previous experiences. Once they've made a decision, it is not easily changed unless it can be shown to be impractical and unworkable. Being able to describe the end product of the change in as much detail as possible helps them get on board with the change.

Production

They tend to be talented at seeing the pieces of a project, how they fit together, and what's missing. They plan and monitor in a thorough, systematic, and careful way, making sure they don't overlook anything that should be done. Approaching tasks in an organized fashion helps them control for things that might go wrong. They will take responsibility for seeing that the details of a task are completed to the agreed-upon standards and on time.

Potential Pitfalls

- Are often so convinced of the steps for doing something, they can miss improvements or variations that are more effective.
- May easily confuse the practical solution with the big-picture systemic solution, thinking a single step can fix the whole system.
- Tend to be so stability oriented that they may insist on procedures for procedures' sake and may hold onto a process beyond its usefulness.

How Are We Doing? How Did We Do?

Since they are keen on monitoring a project to make sure things go right and don't go wrong, they are likely to check in frequently to see if everything is on track. Continuous evaluation and feedback are essential to their sense of commitment to following through until the desired result is achieved.

Who Am I? Who Are You?

Snapshot

Theme is providing, ensuring that physical needs are met. Their talents lie in supporting others and supplying them with what they need. They are genuinely concerned about the welfare of others, making sure they are comfortable and involved. They use their sociability to nurture established institutions. Warm, considerate, thoughtful, and friendly, they want to please and maintain harmonious relationships. They thrive on helping others and bringing people together.

On a Team

- Focus on harmony and involvement; they are often seen as a facilitator/caretaker on a team.
- Can be counted on to follow through and make sure that the necessary resources are available to complete the tasks of the team.
- Expect others to follow the rules and procedures and have a respect for authority that they also expect from others.
- Show genuine concern about the needs of others and provide for their welfare and comfort, helping others feel comfortable with uncomfortable situations.
- Foster positive relationships using cooperation, enthusiasm, and consensus building.
- Organize, prepare for, and remember important events to provide a sense of security and involvement to others.
- Tend to be gently authoritarian and decisive; they give information to prompt and involve rather than directing others' actions.

Potential Blind Spots

- May avoid or smooth over conflict even when issues need to be addressed.
- May be overly sensitive to feedback, often perceiving even developmental feedback as criticism.
- Are sometimes overwhelmed in an attempt to respond to the needs of others and may ignore their own needs to the point of burnout.
- May allow themselves to become overly focused on what "should" be done and then miss the opportunity to be responsive to the needs of a situation.

Who Are We Together?

Relationships

How ESFJs Build Relationships

For them, team relationships are about support and a genuine concern for the welfare of others. Team relationships are about sharing the life of the business, being part of something, and creating a feeling of family. They will often sacrifice for what will benefit others and may put the needs of others ahead of their own to the point of losing themselves to the relationships. When they are aware of hurting other people's feelings, they may skirt heavy issues to maintain equilibrium. At other times they may be quite forthright and appear rude. Then they are surprised when others are offended. They tend to be good listeners who like being involved in the lives of others and helping people with their problems. They put others at ease through their use of self-disclosure.

How ESFJs Deal with Conflict

When conflict occurs, their first concern is that people don't get hurt. First they may have quite an emotional reaction. Then they seek a workable compromise to move matters along and reduce the tension from the conflict. They prefer to keep the mood upbeat, even when dealing with conflict.

To Forge Better Relationships with ESFJs...

Provide a team environment that is open and honest, with attention paid to relationships and personal cooperation. They are most comfortable with routine and a secure, stable work environment. Give them appreciation and meaningful support for who they are and what they do. Give advance notice of change with information about the background and Theorist™e for the change. Time to connect with team members, to engage in mutual problem solving and sharing of ideas, will provide them with opportunities to shine—and, in turn, will bring the team increased harmony and productivity.

Communication

ESFJs Communicate with...

- Stories that convey personal as well as professional information, often showing the pride they take in the successes of others.
- Listening to people's needs and wants.
- Voicing concerns, especially about obstacles that get in the way of people doing well.
- Encouraging people in their participation and involvement.
- A lot of detailed information based on all they've experienced and learned about a subject or about people.

To Communicate with ESFJs...

- Engage in friendly conversations so people get to know each other better.
- Provide specific information, delivered in person or verbally with a warm demeanor.
- Show appreciation for their giving nature and how creative they are in making things "just right."
- Give them time to reflect and analyze the situation but with someone available to talk it through.
- Show a sense of caring about every person on the team.

What Are We Here to Do?

They are likely to interpret the work of the team in terms of the information that is needed for people to do their various jobs, especially in terms of the roles they will fulfill. Getting people to have a shared vision of what needs to be done will not seem like a waste of time to them as long as everyone is involved in the process.

How Are We Going to Do It?

Processes

How ESFJs Approach Doing Work

They want to accept and help others so will focus on making people feel comfortable and involved. They will want to be sure there is time to hear everyone's concerns so that the needs of each person can be accommodated. They are likely to be quick to compromise to move things along. They want to know what the roles are and who is in charge. Important events are to be remembered and milestones acknowledged so successes can be celebrated. They often take on too much and ignore their own needs to help make situations easier for others.

How ESFJs Make Decisions

They often make quick decisions for the welfare of others. When the direction and sequence of a task are clear, they move forward quickly. They will want to keep harmony and consider how decisions will affect people they know and care about.

How ESFJs Respond to Change

Change will not be pursued merely for the sake of change. If a new decision will be more helpful, then they will change direction as needed. They will do a lot of comparing of new information to their personal experiences and all the information they have collected about the people involved.

Production

They willingly provide logistical support where things can be made easier for others. They are inclined to research something thoroughly when it is their responsibility, wanting to make sure they have all the facts and are prepared before they proceed. They often contribute to the production of a team by the way they support others and keep people in touch with each other.

Potential Pitfalls

- May be inattentive to the need to be systematic to control for errors and omissions.
- May find themselves responding to the needs of others and losing track of task details.
- Often act without a well-thought-out strategy.

How Are We Doing? How Did We Do?

They assess how the team is doing through interacting with others and getting a sense of people's involvement. They prefer a group after-action review to the cold data of an assessment.

Temperament: **Stabilizer™** • Interaction Style: **Behind-the-Scenes™** • Cognitive Processes: **Si, Fe, Ti, Ne** | Se, Fi, Te, Ni

Who Am I? Who Are You?

Snapshot

Theme is protecting and caretaking, ensuring their charges are safe from harm. Their talents lie in making sure everything is taken care of so others can succeed and accomplish their goals. Desiring to serve the needs of individuals, they often work long hours. Friendly, respectful, and unassuming, they thrive on serving quietly without fanfare. They are devoted to doing whatever is necessary to ensure shelter and safety, warning about pitfalls and dangers and supporting along the way.

On a Team

- Support and respect others' experiences and talents. They are dedicated to making the team work smoothly and will go the extra mile to make sure it does.
- Care about others in a kind and understanding manner. They focus on harmony and mutual support through teamwork and a sense of belonging.
- Tend to provide structure by having and following a plan.
- Can be consequence oriented and conscientious. They are committed and dedicated to both people and the organization.
- Have a need for stability and security. They expect others to be realistic—following rules, procedures, and protocol without unnecessary and uncalled-for questions.
- Exhibit a quiet, non-threatening, encouraging, and open style.
- Often lead reluctantly. They accept responsibility and pride themselves on being accountable and fulfilling their obligations and assignments.

Potential Blind Spots

- In an effort to satisfy everyone, may have a hard time sticking up for themselves and being assertive.
- Tend to be seen as slow, methodical decision makers and can, at times, be quite stubborn.
- May have little tolerance for ambiguity and require a degree of certainty to feel comfortable.
- Are often seen as serious and concerned; they may over prepare for the worst.

Who Are We Together?

Relationships

How ISFJs Build Relationships

For them, team relationships are about caring about people. They want to get to know people well before sharing a lot with them. They tend to remember a lot of personal detail about people, which establishes close relationships. They want people to be as willing to help as they are. They appreciate space in a conversation for them to reflect and integrate information. When given that space, they appreciate the patience it shows and are likely to make an effort to get back to the team or the individual later.

How ISFJs Deal with Conflict

Conflict is disconcerting for them. It feels disrespectful and emotionally draining. In the face of conflict they tend to do nothing for a while, hoping it will smooth over, then they find a way to bring up issues if they are important. They appreciate being given the time to momentarily withdraw. They will want conflict to be dealt with gently so people don't get hurt.

To Forge Better Relationships with ISFJs...

Provide a structured team environment that clearly defines the roles and responsibilities of the team members with caring and careful attention to detail. Give them positive feedback and acknowledgement, usually quietly and privately. Acknowledge their support as it often goes unnoticed and unrewarded and they can then become discouraged. Be as quietly supportive with them as they are with you. Be patient when they need time to reflect. You can trust them to get back to you later. They take criticism hard, even though they want to improve, because they often see criticism as evidence that they have let you down.

Communication

ISFJs Communicate with...

- Details of what it will take to make something happen so it goes right and doesn't go wrong.
- References to past experiences so resources are not wasted.
- Concerns about making sure all the information is shared; they will seek out others to get that information on the table.
- Information, leaving the decision to accept that information up to the other person.
- A preference for waiting to see what is going on before they speak up.

To Communicate with ISFJs...

- Give them lots of information to filter through a large data bank of life experiences and stored information, looking for what is familiar.
- Be specific, with concrete facts.
- Show them how the decisions will affect the people they know.
- Show the patience to listen to them and to not talk over them.
- Give them time to prepare before being pressed for answers.

What Are We Here to Do?

They are likely to interpret the job or task first in terms of all the detailed steps for making it a success. Then they will look for ways to support the efforts of the team by structuring tasks to make it easy for the team members to get the work done.

How Are We Going to Do It?

Processes

How ISFJs Approach Doing Work

They will focus first on the structure of the situation and role assignments, liking to have roles clearly defined. They want clear lines of authority. Feeling quite responsible for the work of the team, they may be inclined to volunteer for too many jobs when others don't do their share or if no one else signs up. They may have a hard time saying no to requests for help even when they are already overbooked. They will consider the needs of each individual team member, not just the end goal.

How ISFJs Make Decisions

When the situation is familiar, they are likely to recognize the familiarity and make decisions quickly. Sometimes they just go "by the book" to get closure. When making decisions in uncharted territory, they are usually slow and careful in their decision making, preferring to integrate information from many sources and to reflect on matters before they decide.

How ISFJs Respond to Change

Once they've decided on something, changing their minds can be difficult, so give them information early. Help them see the positives in a change, especially as they relate to helping the team function more effortlessly and harmoniously. They want a lot of information, including the Theorist™e for the change, and plenty of time to integrate this new information. When pressed, their first response will likely be no unless they are given time to mull it over.

Production

They provide order and structure and attention to detail. Dependable recordkeepers, they will bring some stability to the processes. They focus on integrating facts and details, and they will often ask questions that bring clarity to what is expected of them, the team, and individual team members. They are often the glue that holds the project and the team together to completion.

Potential Pitfalls

- Can get locked into their perception of what needs to come in what order.
- Can become too anxious and agitated when too much is happening at once.
- Expect things to be the way they were and may miss opportunities.

How Are We Doing? How Did We Do?

They will recognize the importance of quality control and checking to see how the team did. Gathering the data will be natural for them, especially as they see how it can help them improve their output.

ENTJ Strategist Mobilizer™

Temperament: **Theorist™** • Interaction Style: **In-Charge™** • Cognitive Processes: **Te, Ni, Se, Fi** | Ti, Ne, Si, Fe

Who Am I? Who Are You?

Snapshot

Theme is directing and mobilizing. Their talents lie in developing policy, establishing plans, coordinating and sequencing events, and implementing strategy. They excel at directing others in reaching the goals dictated by their strong vision of the organization and thrive on marshaling forces to put plans into action. Natural organization builders, they almost always find themselves taking charge in ineffective situations. They enjoy creating efficiently structured systems and setting priorities to achieve goals.

On a Team

- Typically take charge and lead; they are comfortable making and directing decisions.
- Mentor and empower others in order to focus on developing the talents of the team for long-term results and achievement.
- Mobilize the forces and forge partnerships, maximizing results by utilizing and developing the talents of others.
- Use integrative thinking to incorporate insights and lay out a plan and use differential thinking to critique decisions, plans, and data to prioritize actions.
- Take a systems view of decision making, strategically analyzing to solve problems.
- Are likely to focus on time and task; they direct others to reach goals by efficiently working to get the most done with the least expenditure of resources.
- Tend to be results and action oriented, directing their energy to acquire knowledge and competencies and achieve implementation of their vision.

Potential Blind Spots

- May not praise or give feedback as often as others need it and tend to overlook interpersonal needs of others.
- May be too quick to judge when they see others being "stupid" or not taking responsibility for their actions.
- Can become impatient and overcontrolling, especially when in a hurry for action.
- May not recognize that limitations on a situation can slow progress toward an anticipated outcome.

Who Are We Together?

Relationships

How ENTJs Build Relationships

For them, team relationships are about mutual autonomy and mutual problem solving. They are team players when it's expedient with an element of competition that is geared toward mastery. They want to learn what their teammates know and often see relationships as yet another project to be coordinated to achieve a positive and productive purpose. They enjoy interactions that are going to make them smarter and push them to achieve more. They tend to be straightforward and honest in relationships, which some find refreshing and others find harsh. They are often comfortable initiating relationships yet tend to keep their distance and may be hard to get to know on a personal level. They are usually not very self-disclosing until they trust someone and judge them to be friendly and credible—then they will open up quickly and matter-of-factly.

How ENTJs Deal with Conflict

Conflict for them is yet one more factor to be managed in order to accomplish the goals of the team. They want to take a reasoned approach with little show of emotion. Their first response is to push back and when that doesn't work, they find a way to work around whatever the obstacles to agreement are. They are often seen as more single-solution focused than they actually are and are likely to welcome a good argument. They don't, however, want to waste time covering ground that has already been covered.

To Forge Better Relationships with ENTJs...

Provide a team environment that allows autonomy and fosters independent thought and action. Allow them the freedom to develop strategies and discover new approaches to creating and planning. Provide recognition for achievements and competency from someone they judge as competent and credible. They need logical reasons and rationales for following prescribed procedures. Opportunities to teach and mentor will bring out the best in them.

Temperament: **Theorist™** • Interaction Style: **In-Charge™** • Cognitive Processes: **Te, Ni, Se, Fi** | Ti, Ne, Si, Fe

Communication

ENTJs Communicate with...

- Logical explanations of rationales, goals, and strategies.
- Asking questions to get the information they need to develop a strategy.
- Addressing important issues as they come up.
- Critique aimed at getting work accomplished more efficiently.
- Directives to accomplish goals.

To Communicate with ENTJs...

- Offer logical and reasoned explanations or arguments with a focus on long-range implications and effectiveness.
- Provide straightforward statements of wants, needs, and requirements.
- Pay attention to not wasting time in the interactions.
- Give enough conceptual and factual information so they can formulate a strategy.
- Allow some time to integrate insights and explorations into an effective coordinated plan.

What Are We Here to Do?

They are likely to interpret the job or tasks of the team in terms of what needs to be accomplished to realize the vision. They might not spend much time in articulating the vision in detail so may be a bit impatient with a lot of attempts at clarification.

How Are We Going to Do It?

Processes

How ENTJs Approach Doing Work

Once they have a sense of the strategy needed, they have a tendency to quickly orient to the tasks and the environment in which the tasks must be accomplished so will want to rapidly move to production and getting things accomplished. They tend to make simultaneous assessments of a multitude of data points and quickly analyze, prioritize, and reprioritize as they go. Their whole way of interacting communicates a sense of being in charge, even when they are not. It is important not to misread their drive for accomplishment as single-solution focused. They are often open to improvement.

How ENTJs Make Decisions

They tend to make decisions quickly based on the organization and the implementation of their strategy. Don't confuse their decisiveness with inflexibility. Their pragmatic approach helps them quickly reprioritize actions in line with goals to get something swiftly accomplished.

How ENTJs Respond to Change

The first issue for them is to assess their own competence in the new arena. They tend to fight a change where no convincing rationale and no supporting data are presented. They want to see that the implications of the change have been thought through and that the proposed change will get to the real issues. They tend to respond to new data as it comes up and fit it into the way they've organized and structured their actions.

Production

They tend to be talented at developing long-range strategic plans and at coordinating complex actions to achieve goals. They often take the role of developing policy, establishing plans, coordinating events, and implementing strategy by marshaling and energizing others to get the work done. They are likely to forge partnerships to accomplish complex projects. Their focus will be on mobilizing resources and removing obstacles to get things done.

Potential Pitfalls

- May want to move to production too quickly.
- Can become too insistent when others don't go along with the vision and the strategy they lay out.
- Might ignore the maintenance processes of the group and focus too much on the task processes

How Are We Doing? How Did We Do?

They will want frequent assessments of whether the work is getting done on time so will welcome built-in measures and checkpoints. Evaluation of how the team did as a team may seem a waste of time to them unless it can be shown to relate to getting the work done effectively.

Temperament: **Theorist™** • Interaction Style: **Chart-the-Course™** • Cognitive Processes: **Ni, Te, Fi, Se** | Ne, Ti, Fe, Si

Who Am I? Who Are You?

Snapshot

Theme is strategizing, envisioning, and masterminding. Their talents lie in defining goals, creating detailed plans, and outlining contingencies. They devise strategy, give structure, and establish complex plans to reach distant goals dictated by a strong vision of what is needed in the long run. They thrive on putting theories to work and are open to any and all ideas that can be integrated into the complex systems they seek to understand. They drive themselves hard to master what is needed to make progress toward goals.

On a Team

- Strive for self-mastery; they tend to keep focused on achievement and have high expectations of themselves and others.
- Direct by defining the goal, creating plans, outlining contingencies, and devising strategies.
- Carefully make decisions with a focus on goals and a vision.
- Analyze and synthesize, seeing differences and creating categories. They are devoted to accuracy and precision—the more challenging the problem intellectually, the better they like it.
- May relentlessly drive toward a goal; they employ long-range strategizing to help the team plan and carry out action steps, preferring to delegate the day-to-day operations.
- Prefer privacy and autonomy with time for reflective thinking.
- Can be independent, systems thinkers who naturally grasp the interrelatedness of everything in their organization, using integrative, analytical and often complex thought processes.

Potential Blind Spots

- May be oblivious to the effect of their responses on others; they can be sarcastic and critical of others without realizing the impact.
- Might not give praise and/or feedback as often as others need it and tend to overlook interpersonal needs.
- May be reluctant to delegate, preferring to rely on their own trusted capabilities.
- Appear to believe they can be competent at anything; they may drive themselves and others—and will often be disillusioned when they're not successful.

Who Are We Together?

Relationships

How INTJs Build Relationships

For them, team relationships have purpose—achieving a goal and making progress. They tend to get absorbed in work and enjoy collegial relationships with those who stimulate their thinking. Personal interaction is most often related to moving a project forward, to learning, or to strategizing together. Thus, they can be active team players when it gets the job done more efficiently. When relationship building becomes a deliberate part of their strategy, they willingly make the effort to praise others and put "deposits in the relationship bank."

How INTJs Deal with Conflict

When interpersonal conflict occurs, they will usually withdraw or move on. They want discussions to be calm and reasoned, and highly charged interactions often leave them feeling in complete doubt about what's happening. Relationships with even occasional improvement will be continued, but if they see no progress they will give up, learn from the experience, and move on. When a conflict of vision occurs, they can be stubborn about their own point of view and forge ahead.

To Forge Better Relationships with INTJs...

Provide a team environment that honors their strong need for autonomy and demonstrates respect for individual thoughts and feelings, ideas, and creativity. Provide opportunities for constant evaluation to meet their need for high achievement and competency. Put them in a situation where they can devise and implement long-range strategies aimed at efficient and effective use of the organization's resources.

Communication

INTJs Communicate with...

- Abstract solutions for problem-solving processes.
- A new perspective or vantage point for understanding a situation and a desired result.
- A vision of where to go and a plan for how to get there.
- Logical explanations that build up to an argument that supports their conceptualization.
- Questions to check on progress toward achieving the goal.

To Communicate with INTJs...

- Appreciate the complexity of thought behind their solutions.
- Offer logical arguments, especially those that point out the long-range implications.
- Be direct, matter-of-fact, and explicit.
- Demonstrate openness to seeing the vision.
- Give them time to integrate new information and reconceptualize their thinking if what is presented is very different from their vision and to build a new premise for their logic.

What Are We Here to Do?

They are likely to interpret the job or tasks of the teams in terms of their vision of the future of what the job or tasks contribute to, weighing current and future goals. They will want to be sure that the vision is well defined and may spend time researching to have enough information to formulate the desired result.

How Are We Going to Do It?

Processes

How INTJs Approach Doing Work

They may seem quite disengaged from the group as they gather lots of information about the why and the how of the situation. They will want time to analyze data and integrate information to create an internal map that gives them points of reference. Then the map is laid out and if no progress is being made, directives are given to get movement. Before a meeting they want an agenda, or at least a rough idea of what is to be accomplished.

How INTJs Make Decisions

They tend to make strategic decisions rather quickly as they compare new information to their vision. They can react in a very passionate way to the select principles or activities they find important. Concrete, logistical decisions often frustrate them or go unmade. They tend to critique the process used to think about a problem rather than focusing on the problem itself or the specifics.
They may present several options for action, each with its own pros and cons and each thought through to its ultimate consequences.

How INTJs Respond to Change

When dealing with change, the issue becomes one of how congruent the change is with their vision. They tend to be so strongly convinced of their vision and a sense of being right that they find it hard to see how they could have been wrong. When this is the case, they need to see incontrovertible evidence and well-grounded logic to reconceptualize their vision and embrace the change.

Production

They tend to be talented at putting theories to work by mapping out feasible events, developing agendas, and building models. They use systems thinking and deductive reasoning to synthesize and organize ideas. They will often lay out this map and then be the ones who check the points of reference along the way.

Potential Pitfalls

- May spend too much time developing the vision and doing research and miss the window of opportunity.
- May become impatient with a trial-and-error approach because of their focus on progress and avoiding failure.
- Can put too much faith in, or infer too much from, one or two instances/observations.

How Are We Doing? How Did We Do?

They will want frequent checks for progress toward the goal, wanting to be sure the team is on track to accomplishing the tasks in line with the vision. They will want to analyze what really happened to incorporate that information into revisions of the vision and plans to achieve that vision.

Temperament: **Theorist™** • Interaction Style: **Get-Things-Going™** • Cognitive Processes: **Ne, Ti, Fe, Si** | Ni, Te, Fi, Se

Who Am I? Who Are You?

Snapshot

Theme is inventing, finding ingenious solutions to people and technical problems. Their talents lie in developing ideas into functional and innovative applications that are the first of their kind. They thrive on finding new ways to use theories to make systems more efficient and people better off. Hungry for new projects, they have faith in their ability to instantly come up with new approaches that will work. They are engineers of human relationships and systems as well as in the more scientific and technological domains.

On a Team

- Bring high energy to projects. They are adept at mobilizing others, bringing team members together in challenging and stimulating discovery.
- Use a multi-focused analysis to see differences and create categories that help the team find unusual, creative solutions to problems.
- Can be project oriented. They use their skills in synthesis and design to improvise and invent.
- Often build and engineer theoretical models to address complex systems issues.
- Typically communicate the general outline of the vision, ask others for input, and then let everyone follow his or her own interests toward the goal.
- Engineer relationships, often making the first move to establish a connection—especially when it gives them an opportunity to generate or share ideas and insights in their ongoing quest to constantly learn, create, and achieve.
- Often function as trailblazers, fostering change and the development of long-range strategies to accomplish that change or the design of new products and revision of current ones.

Potential Blind Spots

- Given their abstract random thinking, may miss concrete data, especially when generating ideas.
- Might jump to strategic problem solving before the team is ready and then be surprised when others are still processing input and ideas.
- Often look at the world so analytically and unconventionally that they may forget about social conventions and protocol.
- Sometimes find that the mutual sharing of ideas becomes competitive and not as much fun for colleagues.

Who Are We Together?

Relationships

How ENTPs Build Relationships

For them, team relationships are about generating and sharing ideas. They are assertive in initiating relationships and there is usually an easy initial connection. They bring people together for interesting conversations. They want them to be at ease and to stimulate lively debate. They are good at connecting and aligning with people, getting to know them and sharing interests and activities. They are often a catalyst for the team, seeing the potential in others' activities and perspectives. With their flood of new ideas and creative, unusual solutions they may be viewed by team members as out of control and into too many "grand" ideas at once; not realizing the perceptions of others, they may not verbalize the strategy behind their multi-focusing.

How ENTPs Deal with Conflict

It may appear that they like conflict since they often engage in rather heated discussions to bring clarity and a more comprehensive understanding to the issues. When a conflict occurs, they will try to keep the conversation going and reframe what is going on, often commenting on the conversation and the direction it is taking. This can be misperceived as manipulative when it is really intended to keep things moving in a positive direction by working through conflict to get to an agreement.

To Forge Better Relationships with ENTPs...

Provide a team environment that is non-routine and that allows entrepreneurial explorations and creative approaches to problem solving. Give them the opportunity to share insights about life's possibilities and to achieve success with those ideas. They need challenge, intellectual stimulation, interaction with others, autonomy, and opportunities to invent and improvise solutions to complex problems.

Communication

ENTPs Communicate with...

- A multitude of options for things to do and multiple ways to see things.
- Inferences and hypotheses about what is going on and why it is going on.
- Abstract, somewhat impressionistic information of where a project needs to go or what needs to be done.
- Insights about life's possibilities and effective strategies.
- Devil's advocate arguments.

To Communicate with ENTPs...

- Provide lots of new information, other ideas, and other options.
- Actively engage in brainstorming and decision-making processes.
- Be open to multiple models.
- Trust in their instincts to recognize strategic opportunities.
- Show appreciation for their often radical ideas.

What Are We Here to Do?

They are likely to interpret the job or tasks of the team in open-ended multiple ways. They quite likely will want to brainstorm and discuss exactly what the team is supposed to do rather than accept a definition from somewhere else.

How Are We Going to Do It?

Processes

How ENTPs Approach Doing Work

They will want a fair amount of autonomy and freedom to try out some of the many creative solutions they generate. They won't settle for a quick fix but want to come up with efficient solutions. While they give a lot of attention to having a strategy, they also work at maintaining good relationships. They want a lot of involvement by everyone on the team.

How ENTPs Make Decisions

They tend to make decisions rather quickly in response to new information regarding the system or the potential for making a complex model accessible and usable. They quickly gather conceptual information to sort into categories, set criteria, and move to a metaposition with principles about how to problem solve. Decisions are based first on new possibilities that will get the job done and then on theoretical accuracy.

How ENTPs Respond to Change

When a change is needed, they are likely to quickly move to brainstorming new ideas and options for doing things differently. This sometimes means they will not readily embrace a change as it is put forth but will try to improve upon it. They can become resistant to a change if they get locked into their sense of how it could be in the future or what the major trends are. Since they want to be involved in improving things, they often can get unstuck by more brainstorming.

Production

Strongly motivated by challenges, they tend to be talented at generating unusual solutions that resolve problems rather than just fix them. They are inventive at finding solutions to people and technical problems. One of their major contributions is to develop ideas into functional and innovative applications. They can often possess a mix of creativity and technical expertise.

Potential Pitfalls

- May show their devotion to accuracy and precision by splitting hairs and rejecting or challenging anything that appears not to be well thought out.
- Enthusiastically generate many ideas, strategies, and models yet may avoid the structure and attention to detail needed for implementation.
- Tend to metacommunicate and engineer relationships, which can get in the way of getting the work done.

How Are We Doing? How Did We Do?

They will typically trust their instincts about what is working and what is not working before they trust data.

Temperament: **Theorist™** • Interaction Style: **Behind-the-Scenes™** • Cognitive Processes: **Ti, Ne, Si, Fe** | Te, Ni, Se, Fi

Who Am I? Who Are You?

Snapshot

Theme is designing and configuring. Their talents lie in grasping the underlying principles of something and defining its essential qualities. They seek to define precisely and bring coherence to systems based on the pattern of organization that is naturally there. They easily notice inconsistencies. They enjoy elegant theories and models for their own sake and for use in solving technical and human problems. Interested in theorizing, analyzing, and learning, they thrive on exploring, understanding, and explaining how the world works.

On a Team

- Design and theorize; they quickly grasp underlying principles and define essential qualities of any issue or problem.
- Tend to analyze everything; they point out differences and develop categories to help them strategize and map out all feasible possibilities.
- Are likely to wordsmith to get precision in the expression of what they and others want to communicate.
- Help the team get to the essence of a problem by clearly defining the situation and seeing connections.
- Engineer connections—help connect people with ideas and information as well as network people to people—usually around expertise.
- Generate ideas, see patterns and inconsistencies, and help others grasp the variables of an issue.
- Typically provide autonomy and options, assuming others want it as much as they do.

Potential Blind Spots

- Are often impatient with errors, covering ground already covered, and other signs of inaccuracy and inefficiency.
- May be seen as not caring or being a team player when they detach to analyze, critique, and problem solve.
- May be seen by team members as being too theoretical or too skeptical, too rigid with one idea.
- May lose focus by spending too much time playing with many ideas.

Who Are We Together?

Relationships

How INTPs Build Relationships

For them, team relationships are about sharing expertise. They want to have a joint area of interest and competence to share and energetically engage in collaborative problem solving and strategizing. They typically seek out relationships so they can have different thoughts and experiences yet often feel they lack interpersonal skills. In fact, their relationships can become competitive and may interfere with the intellectual needs that drove them to seek the relationships in the first place. When they recognize that their tendency to precisely define words, clarify ideas, and point out inconsistencies can get in the way of team relationships, they willingly learn to remember to thank and praise teammates for their contributions before they critique them.

How INTPs Deal with Conflict

The disruption that comes from team conflict keeps them from thinking clearly, so they avoid confrontation unless it is absolutely necessary. They might avoid conflict for too long, hoping it will go away. While they like a lively debate of ideas, when it becomes personal they can become noncommunicative until they can see a way to work with the conflict to resolve it.

To Forge Better Relationships with INTPs...

Provide a team environment that is calm and conflict-free and where consultative rather than hierarchical relationships are the norm. Give them enough freedom to reflect on how things work, to generate ideas, and to see connections and patterns. Offer them opportunities to direct their energy toward acquisition of knowledge and competence. To gain their commitment and compliance, give them the logic, rationale, or proof behind standard operating procedures, conventions, and protocols.

Communication

INTPs Communicate with...

- The guiding principles that are essential for accuracy and the best result possible.
- Their expertise and knowledge based on their models, their sense of what has worked in the past, and statements of principles.
- Clarifying comments that define a problem.
- Information about what the problem is and possible solutions.
- Critique of things that are not internally consistent and coherent.

To Communicate with INTPs...

- Provide new information that presents other workable options.
- Be internally consistent in your logic.
- Engage in friendly discourse that involves logical debate about theories and models and ways they could be improved.
- Offer rationales for why things are the way they are, how things work, and why they don't work.
- Give them credit for their ideas, which are often very quietly given and thus credit is overlooked.

What Are We Here to Do?

They are likely to focus on getting a clear definition of what the job or task is and what it involves. They will look to define the guiding principles so there is agreement on what is to be done and why.

How are we going to do it?

Processes

How INTPs Approach Doing Work

They are inclined to first analyze a situation, seeking to understand the principles that apply. Then they will want to integrate all kinds of information from a variety of sources. They tend to focus on how things work, why they work that way, and what makes them not work and then try to come up with an elegant solution that really solves the problem. They want the autonomy to find the right theories, models, or explanations and then to share the information they have found.

How INTPs Make Decisions

They tend to quickly decide on the accuracy of theories and frameworks, yet they labor over the accurate expression of ideas. They may avoid decisions regarding an action or establishing order and structure. Logistical decisions are often seen as trivial and either slighted or labored over. Interpersonal decisions are made to avoid disruption and to keep the peace.

How INTPs Respond to Change

They are likely to say they are not resistant to change since they are constantly developing and revising their designs and approaches. However, they do tend to resist change that appears illogical and seems to violate principles. Change that means changing their habitual way of doing routine tasks is also hard for them, especially if a big learning curve is involved. Helping them see how what they are doing isn't effective and relating the change to progress in the grand scheme of things and its strategic purpose will help.

Production

They tend to be talented at bringing clarity to defining problems, analyzing and pointing out differences and developing categories. They devise systems of thought and efficient actions that can be directed toward the work of the team. Generating ideas and seeing connections energizes them and provides the information they seek to continually redesign and improve a product or the process.

Potential Pitfalls

- May not have a realistic sense of what it takes to put their ideas and designs into place, either logistically or timewise.
- In the service of getting things just right, may tend to make them more complex than they need to be.
- Can dampen enthusiasm and involvement with continual critiquing, even though it is in the best interest of the team and the project.

How Are We Doing? How Did We Do?

They assess outcomes based on how consistently they match applicable principles and models. They are quite likely to find flaws in data-gathering methods if a variety of variables are not accounted for. They trust their own sense of what worked and what didn't above the data.

Temperament: **Catalyst™** • Interaction Style: **In-Charge™** • Cognitive Processes: **Fe, Ni, Se, Ti** | Fi, Ne, Si, Te

Who Am I? Who Are You?

Snapshot

Theme is mentoring, leading people to achieve their potential and become more of who they are. Their talents lie in empathizing with profound interpersonal insight and in influencing others to learn, grow, and develop. They lead using their exceptional communication skills, enthusiasm, and warmth to gain cooperation toward meeting the ideals they hold for the individual or the organization. Catalysts who draw out the best in others, they thrive on empathic connections. Frequently, they are called on to help others with personal problems.

On a Team

- Are often talented at drawing out the best in others, providing team members with camaraderie, mutual support, and a commitment to the overall team effort.
- Tend to take leadership positions and are looked on by others as leaders, even if not officially the team leader.
- Use their communication skills, enthusiasm, and warmth to gain cooperation, collaboration, and consensus.
- Operate as catalysts who energize the team with enthusiasm and humor.
- Tune into the climate of the organization and the team.
- Are likely to mentor people to achieve their potential through coaching, encouragement, and positive feedback.
- Encourage and honor diversity to use the resources of the team, pointing out the unique gifts individuals bring to a team.

Potential Blind Spots

- May get lost in relationships and overburdened with problems of others, focusing too much on harmony, then get off task.
- Can be overly fixed on their vision or interpretation of something.
- Tend to work in bursts of energy that may not coincide with the needs of the team.
- May have a hard time separating from their ideal of teamwork and being objective.

Who Are We Together?

Relationships

How ENFJs Build Relationships

For them, team relationships are about connecting and mentoring. They see potential in others and are usually good at spotting talent within a team. They know people need lots of attention and commitment and want the same in return. Nurturing relationships is vital to them and they want that on their teams, so they require a sense of connection, to feel known, understood, needed, reassured, and praised in the team environment. They tend to invest a lot in relationships, which sometimes can create a standard on the team that others may not be able to live up to. Yet teammates are likely to feel at ease with them and open up. Tending to be open and sharing, they expect others to self-disclose to help build relationships as well as resolve issues. They are likely to see extreme attention to a task and an abrupt style in others as neglecting the relationships. Such communication often leads to hurt feelings, which they nurse internally.

How ENFJs Deal with Conflict

When conflict occurs within the team, they will want to talk about the problems and heal the conflict before going on. When there is too much conflict and ongoing disharmony, they have a tendency to withdraw. They hate when people are demeaned or mistreated and will stand up for someone who is.

To Forge Better Relationships with ENFJs...

Provide an open, harmonious, and sharing environment where they and others can feel safe to self-disclose. Give them time and space to develop logical arguments or explanations. Give them lots of genuine positive feedback because they value the approval of others and often feel undervalued. Provide opportunities for interaction, both task related and social. Most of all, frame the work of the team in a context of some higher purpose.

Communication

ENFJs Communicate with...

- Warmly enthusiastic sharing of visions, values, and purpose for individuals and for the team.
- Information about the impact on people, their well-being, and their relationships.
- A fresh view of how things can be.
- Support, appreciation, and praise.
- Feedback on how results or progress match with what's hoped for.

To Communicate with ENFJs...

- Give them sincere appreciation for their unique contributions.
- Be direct, yet show kindness.
- Demonstrate a willingness to see potential in their vision and an opportunity to generate possibilities toward a plan.
- Show warmth and acceptance of who they are.
- Provide time for them to sort through everything and readjust their vision.

What Are We Here to Do?

They are likely to interpret the job or tasks of the team in terms of their vision for the future and what that will mean to the people involved. They tend to work to get everyone communicating so there is a shared vision of the job.

How Are We Going to Do It?

Processes

How ENFJs Approach Doing Work

They will want ample opportunity to communicate and share values and the vision. In the work of the team they will seek ways to help team members grow and develop. Often they will notice potential in team members that might be ignored and then they will work to find ways to bring out that potential for the benefit of the team and the individual. Defining and assigning roles is one way they accomplish this.

How ENFJs Make Decisions

They tend to make quick decisions when a task needs to be done and want to get it accomplished right away. When given new information, they tend to withdraw mentally to visualize the impact of new information on the people involved and the vision.

How ENFJs Respond to Change

When a change happens, they will first check the change for its effect on their vision of the identity and integrity of the group/team/organization and the individuals in it. If it doesn't match their vision, they'll fight the change. They will need time alone to integrate new data and incorporate it into a new vision. They will often want to research information to help others deal with a change.

Production

They tend to be talented at seeing potential in others and mentoring them to achieve it. They are likely to take on the role of facilitating goal accomplishment through cooperation and considering all options. Often more gets done on the team because of this mentoring and fostering of a cooperative attitude.

Potential Pitfalls

- Can get so caught up in developing the potential of teammates, they lose sight of the work of the team.
- Sometimes have difficulty separating their interests from the interests of others so are easily swayed by what is in the best interest of the group, even if it is not in their own best interest.
- May spend too much time communicating and can feel desperate when faced with a time/task deadline and too many problems.

How Are We Doing? How Did We Do?

They tend to constantly monitor the sense of cooperation among team members and will welcome measures of accomplishment.

Temperament: **Catalyst™** • Interaction Style: **Chart-the-Course™** • Cognitive Processes: **Ni, Fe, Ti, Se** | Ne, Fi, Te, Si

Who Am I? Who Are You?

Snapshot

Theme is foresight. They use their insights to deal with complexity in issues and people, often with a strong sense of "knowing" before others know themselves. Their talents lie in developing and guiding people. They trust their inspirations and visions, using them to help others. They thrive on helping others resolve deep personal and ethical dilemmas. Private and complex, they bring a quiet enthusiasm and industry to projects that are part of their vision.

On A Team

- Inspire others with a positive, enthusiastic approach, helping them find their purpose or meaning.
- Like the connectedness of being on a team, yet they love independent projects that they can see progress on.
- Can be organized and will often organize the team if no one else will, leading quietly by example in a predictable, orderly, and very personal way.
- Often have a strong sense of purpose, following their vision of how "it" will be. This makes them look very task oriented to fellow team members.
- Show loyalty to the team, individuals, and the organization.
- Tend to use insight and interpersonal warmth to organize, counsel, inspire, and teach. Unfortunately, sometimes team members don't want to hear all the insights they have.
- Often use symbols and metaphors to bridge differences within the team and connect people.

Potential Blind Spots

- Can be seen as distant by others as they try to move the task along and/or manage their own emotions.
- May let go of their own needs and lose sight of their own identity, leading to eventual burnout.
- Might focus on growth and development of themselves or others so much they get off task and lose a sense of perspective.
- May disconnect when the team loses the vision, thereby losing their opportunity to influence the group.

Who Are We Together?

Relationships

How INFJs Build Relationships

For them, team relationships are about supporting human potential. They often show a talent for developing and guiding people, so putting them in a coaching role on the team benefits all. It is often painful, however, when they offer insights or advice and teammates choose not to take it. Others may see them as either more outgoing or more critical than they are. They often come to team relationships with pre-established expectations but are willing to change if met with new information or new teammates. They quickly pick up on insincerity and withdraw if someone on the team is superficial or obviously doesn't care.

How INFJs Deal with Conflict

They typically don't like conflict but won't avoid it if it can improve relationships or lead to growth. Therefore, they are likely catalysts for airing team issues within the group. When conflict occurs, they first withdraw to sort it out, then seek to have a conversation where the conflict can be addressed. They realize the importance of keeping their emotions in check and not saying things that can damage relationships.

To Forge Better Relationships with INFJs...

Provide a team environment that focuses on people and their needs. Try to create an open, honest, and sincere relationship with them and help them create that kind of relationship with others on the team. Give them genuine, meaningful feedback, which does not always have to be positive, to let them know you are aware of their contributions. Most of all, frame the work of the team as having a meaningful purpose that goes beyond everyday routine.

Communication

INFJs Communicate with...

- Thoughtful sharing of insights, especially about people—their talents and contributions.
- Foresights about what will happen.
- A sense of the profound significance of something and the interrelatedness of events, ideas, and relationships.
- Meaningful symbols and metaphors that help build bridges between people.
- Supportive and positive feedback as well as criticism when it is important.

To Communicate with INFJs...

- Provide a clear sense of where the team is going and progress being made.
- Convey a sense of the purpose and a new perspective, and talk about the future.
- Show a willingness to untangle the complexities of interpersonal issues.
- Be open to the insights they bring and insights they have.
- Give them time to integrate new information, especially if it is counter to what they have foreseen will happen.

What Are We Here to Do?

They are likely to interpret the tasks of the team in terms of the vision of the future that the tasks contribute to. They will especially focus on getting a clear vision of each task itself.

How Are We Going to Do It?

Processes

How INFJs Approach Doing Work

They have a tendency to spend a fair amount of up-front reflection time to mentally get a sense of where the project and the team are going so will likely disengage from the group momentarily. They want a course of action or reference points to help team members know when they are on track. They see the value in defining roles so tasks can get done and matching the right team members with the tasks to accomplish the vision. Once underway, they are quite likely to be very time and task focused unless the team gets derailed or people clearly need attending to in order to be productive.

How INFJs Make Decisions

They tend to make decisions rather quickly if new information matches the vision. If it doesn't, they will want time to integrate the information into their vision and adjust the vision or reject the information. They might be prone to inaction when they get overwhelmed with the physical realities of a situation or when they have no idea of what the next step should be.

How INFJs Respond to Change

When a change doesn't match their vision of what is going to happen, they must trust that others are really looking out for the good of the people. This will help them adjust their vision, especially if accompanied by a good argument with a strong rationale and with new insights and evidence.

Production

They tend to be talented at developing and guiding people. They see every opportunity as a growth opportunity, yet they personally do not have to be involved for the growth to happen. They will want to have the time to reflect and envision a desired result, then engage in practical problem solving to realize the vision. When they have a sense of what to do, they are quick to get it done. If they see no progress, they may succumb to discouragement and self-criticism.

Potential Pitfalls

- Once they get a sense of what needs to be done, may be too time and task oriented to take in new information.
- May trust their insights so much they may avoid getting the data that could make the process or product better.
- May get such a strong impression of something that it feels very real to them, then they may have difficulty communicating it to the rest of the team and become overly critical if their vision isn't being realized.

How Are We Doing? How Did We Do?

They will want frequent checks for progress toward the goal, wanting to be sure the team is on track.

Temperament: **Catalyst™** • Interaction Style: **Get-Things-Going™** • Cognitive Processes: **Ne, Fi, Te, Si** | Ni, Fe, Ti, Se

Who Am I? Who Are You?

Snapshot

Theme is inspiration, both of themselves and others. Their talents lie in grasping profound significance, revealing truths, and motivating others. Very perceptive of others' hidden motives and purposes, they are interested in everything about individuals and their stories as long as they are genuine. They have a contagious enthusiasm for causes that further good and develop latent potential and have the same zeal for revealing dishonesty and inauthenticity. Frequently, they are moved to enthusiastically communicate their "message."

On a Team

- Often become the spokesperson for other teammates for what is needed most, to voice the unspoken meanings they so easily pick up.
- Keep communication channels open among team members to make the best of a situation.
- Tend to engage team members by listening, facilitating, training, motivating, recruiting, counseling, and understanding others' perspectives.
- Demonstrate an understanding of others that fosters collaborative teamwork and yet encourages individual contributions to the team.
- Lead with their energy and enthusiasm for causes, engaging and involving others, with an eye to what is needed most for the team or the organization.
- Get involved with teammates on a personal level, inspiring and helping them to find happiness and well-being and to reach their full potential.
- Focus on others' concerns, listening and mediating when differences threaten the team.

Potential Blind Spots

- Often instantly like people or not, and liking the people they are with is important—especially on a team. When they don't like someone, they may have a hard time engaging with the person.
- Can be surprised when others miss what seems quite apparent to them or when others don't pick up on what they thought they were saying.
- Can easily become bored with routine, becoming distressed and struggling to carry out ongoing projects to completion.
- Tend to focus on pursuing a task via interaction, exploring too many related tangents and then missing the target.

Who Are We Together?

Relationships

How ENFPs Build Relationships

For them, team relationships are about being on the same wavelength as others, getting involved at a personal, empathic level. They read and mirror other people's moods and intended meanings, so team members often feel perfectly understood by them. They usually establish rapport instantly in a way that uniquely connects with another person. Discussing and resolving deep issues is important to them. Often sparking such conversations, they are frequently catalysts for change, moving the team along in its development. In a team meeting, they are often at the center of attention without being the topic of conversation. They want everyone to engage and on the team will work endlessly to get engagement, yet they find it hard to communicate their own needs or ideas and forget to talk about themselves.

How ENFPs Deal with Conflict

While they prefer happy and upbeat relationships, when conflict occurs, they usually want to engage in a dialog to work it out. Nothing upsets them more than when a teammate refuses to talk through a situation they've decided is worth resolving. Since they want to resolve the conflict and keep the team connected and moving along, they are usually willing to compromise if a true win-win agreement can't be worked out.

To Forge Better Relationships with ENFPs...

Provide a team environment that is genuine and understanding of their uniqueness and the importance of people-oriented issues. Provide minimal insistence on rules, systems, and procedures. Honor their need to authentically live with themselves, which will drive their decisions. If you don't take their expressions and contributions seriously, they may withdraw. Most of all, acknowledge their ideas and help them work through them.

Communication

ENFPs Communicate with...

- Enthusiastic sharing of insights to get people involved and projects moving along.
- General impressions of what they see is really going on.
- A multitude of possibilities, potentials, and ideas for making things better.
- Voicing of issues and unspoken messages.
- Inspiration and facilitation.

To Communicate with ENFPs...

- Give them recognition for their enthusiastic energy and their unique talents and contributions.
- Respond to information they give, especially about what they want but haven't asked for directly.
- Show a willingness to engage in interaction and dialog.
- Maintain frequent contact, keeping them involved in what is going on.
- Provide a sense of what things mean in the grand scheme and how it will be good for people.

What Are We Here to Do?

They will likely ask, "What needs to get started and who needs to be involved?" They will get an impression that something needs to happen or an important ideal needs to be reached, then they will start moving toward it and adjusting along the way.

How Are We Going to Do It?

Processes

How ENFPs Approach Doing Work

They have a tendency to see a lot of options and will want to brainstorm and explore those options as they come up. They prefer to have the choice of approaching tasks creatively rather than by the book. Liking people they work with will be just as important as the work, so they will want to spend some time getting to know people—what people's roles are and how everyone relates. They are likely to get a quick impression of what needs to be done and then enthusiastically get people involved in getting it underway.

How ENFPs Make Decisions

They tend to make quick decisions in response to opportunities that match the "ideal"; otherwise, they may deliberate over choosing the one right thing. All the options they see can overwhelm them if they are not thoroughly in touch with their values and how those values line up with the goals of the team/organization. On a team, they will want to reach consensual decisions as often as possible.

How ENFPs Respond to Change

When a change fits with their values and their vision, they jump right in, suggesting ideas of how to make the change happen. Often they seek change to stimulate growth; however, they can resist change that seems to go against personal, team, or organizational identity. Sometimes they get stuck in their expectations of what should happen based on earlier experiences. Then they need to hear a new perspective in order to feel new excitement about the change.

Production

They tend to be talented at grasping profound significance, revealing truths, and motivating others, which makes a big contribution to production along with the tasks they do themselves. Their approach to getting work done will likely be to grasp the overview quickly, connect with others, and jump in enthusiastically, unless the task involves a great deal of routine that they are not committed to. They often find common ground in divergent perspectives so that all are incorporated in an end result.

Potential Pitfalls

- May become impatient when ideas cannot be implemented as quickly as they'd like, then become easily discouraged.
- May assume they know what needs to be done and then forge ahead without checking for strategic, logistical, and tactical necessities.
- May get a flurry of ideas and not be able to focus.

How Are We Doing? How Did We Do?

They will like the discussions of an after-action review process for the interaction, involvement, and improvement. However, they may not see the need to take more quantitative measures of how the team is doing, unless they can be applied to improving future team processes.

Who Am I? Who Are You?

Snapshot

Theme is advocacy and integrity. Their talents lie in helping people clarify issues, values, and identity. They support anything that allows the unfolding of a person. They encourage growth and development with quiet enthusiasm. Loyal advocates and champions, they care deeply about their causes and a few special people. They are interested in contemplating life's mysteries, virtues, and vices in their search for wholeness. They thrive on healing conflicts and taking people to the center of themselves.

On a Team

- Identify strongly with others, bringing to light intentions, strengths, needs, and motivators to help build on those strengths and overcome weaknesses so the team can achieve its goal.
- Bring harmonizing people skills to the team—listening, facilitating, motivating, and counseling.
- Can be perceived as quietly people oriented, championing the underdog and other worthwhile causes and encouraging individuals to achieve.
- Listen deeply to team members, helping them clarify their identity, their wants, and their needs.
- May be seen as fun and playful yet with serious intent. They are supportive, caring, and participative.
- Enjoy bringing together different ideas, finding what's similar in order to reach the goal.
- Tend to have minimal focus on rules and procedures that are seen to inhibit freedom and self-expression.

Potential Blind Spots

- Might concentrate on deeper issues in relationships or the team process and get off task, losing a sense of perspective.
- Frequently reflect on how to "be" in a relationship and may miss the moment for connecting with a teammate.
- Can have difficulty with structure and bureaucracy, fearing it will shut down possibilities and potentials.
- May become overzealous about a value, finding it difficult to acknowledge another's point of view and appearing righteous and arrogant.

Who Are We Together?

Relationships

How INFPs Build Relationships

For them, team relationships are about making space for others to participate fully. They like to help others accept themselves and believe in themselves. They have a talent for reading between the lines, hearing what hasn't been said, and getting a sense of what needs to be said and done. They want others to have a sense of purpose and ethics and to be congruent with these in their behavior. Knowing people's intentions helps them feel comfortable with their relationships on the team. They honor and accept as valid the communication or feeling teammates express when sharing something that is important to them—and expect others to do the same. They often relate through stories and metaphors, bridging differences by emphasizing and building on similarities and providing gentle encouragement. Sharing beliefs is important to them, yet it is sometimes difficult for them to put into words the things that really matter to them. They tend to do a lot of mental rehearsal in problem solving so may appear quiet and withdrawn in team meetings.

How INFPs Deal with Conflict

Their first response to conflict is usually to wait and see what is involved. Then they will go with the flow of what is happening, working to bring out all sides of an issue and resolve deeper issues that are likely at the root of the conflict. The worst kind of conflict to them occurs when their values are challenged as not worthy or when they feel a sense of betrayal. They want people, themselves included, to be listened to with respect and openness.

To Forge Better Relationships with INFPs...

Provide a team environment that holds a sense of integrity and opportunities for fostering wholeness, harmony, mental health, and growth in others. Be sure to validate and affirm them as individuals. Give them the flexibility to capitalize on bursts of energy and not be berated for the lulls in between. Recognize the value in their impressions rather than force them to be explicit. Let them work alone as they need to, yet provide them with opportunities to meaningfully connect with others. Most of all, help them find personal meaning in the team project.

Communication

INFPs Communicate with...

- Ideas for ways things can be in the future.
- Listening to others' dreams, visions, and goals.
- Clarifying questions to harmonize values and purpose.
- Information about implications, subtle meanings, and points of view others may overlook.
- Strong statements of belief, supporting evidence, data, and history for those issues they feel strongly about.

To Communicate with INFPs...

- Give them an opportunity to gather impressions and get a sense of how people feel.
- Be authentic and sincere in interactions.
- Show a willingness to non-judgmentally and enthusiastically listen to their vision and values.
- Provide a lot of information with time to reflect and integrate.
- Demonstrate a respectful attitude toward everyone concerned.

What Are We Here to Do?

They are likely to assess the job or tasks of the team in terms of the congruency between the job and the values. If they don't match, then they are likely to want to adjust the definition of the work so it is congruent, seeking more information to get a more ideal result.

How Are We Going to Do It?

Processes

How INFPs Approach Doing Work

They have a tendency to go with the flow until they have enough information to integrate into a complete picture. They like to play with a lot of ideas. If they get a sense that things are not going in the right direction, they will make suggestions to try to turn the situation around. Their usually gentle informing style is amazingly powerful. When they are dedicated to a purpose, they can be tireless in their search for supporting information and data.

How INFPs Make Decisions

They tend to make fast decisions about whether something or someone is congruent or not but may decide slowly about what actions to take and what direction to pursue. They want to be sure they've got all the information, and then once they get a clear sense that important values are not violated and actions will be congruent with those values, then they act quickly. Inaction may result if personal values conflict with the external demands for action or if many differing values have to be reconciled and unified in one decision.

How INFPs Respond to Change

When change is necessary, they tend to hold tight to a kind of artistic control, checking for congruity with values. They are open to change when they have some creative input into the process and they feel the change will increase the likelihood of an even higher quality outcome. They will want to be sure everyone's voice is heard and consensus is reached wherever possible.

Production

They tend to be talented at facilitative listening and knowing what is behind what is said. Thus they often engage in clarifying issues that get in the way of being productive. One of their major contributions to production will be as a catalyst to others and as a healing force within the team. When they are on board with a project, they work hard to make it happen.

Potential Pitfalls

- May become so absorbed in a project that they lose sight of what is taking place around them and appear to be unfocused.
- May be less productive if they feel people are not being treated with dignity and not getting their needs met.
- May resist the structure needed for effectively managing projects.

How Are We Doing? How Did We Do?

They will usually look to their impressions of the interpersonal processes to see if the team is functioning well and to assess how well the team did with respect to the goal. When more formal assessment is required, they are likely to see its benefit.

Applying the Five Essential Issues

The worksheets in this section are to help you and your team apply the basics of effective teamwork. Use the worksheets to have discussions with your teammates and come to some agreement about how you want to work together, how you will make decisions, and how you will handle conflict. All questions on the worksheets may not be relevant to every team and there are likely more questions that could be asked. Use these questions to begin applying the five essentials to your team.

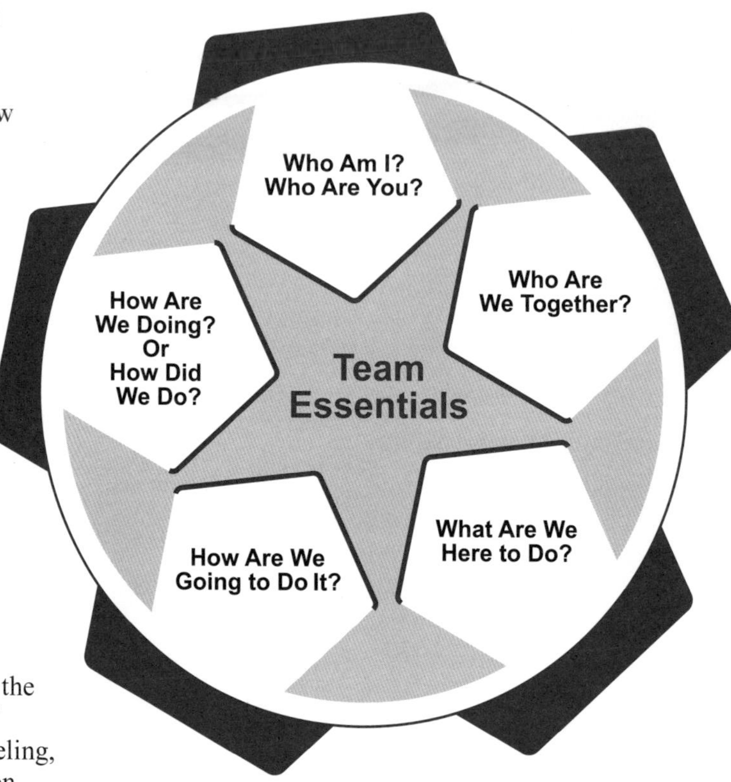

To look at the issue of Who We Are Together we use a tool called Mapping the Team. Because different models are used with the 16 Personality Types we have provided four different ways to map the team. We expect you will reference the pages that refer to the models you are most familiar with. However, you may also find value in looking at the other models.

1. Mapping the Team Using Type Preferences, pages 40-41, provides a look at the impact on the team of the four dichotomies of Extraversion/Introversion, Sensing/iNtuiting, Thinking/Feeling, and Judging/Perceiving as well as the Function Pairs of ST, SF, NT, and NF.

2. Mapping the Team Using Temperament, pages 42-43, provides a look at the impact on the team of the four temperament patterns of Improviser™, Stabilizer™, Theorist™ and Catalyst™ as well as the temperament dynamics of Abstract-Concrete language and Affiliative versus Pragmatic roles.

3. Mapping the Team Using Interaction Styles, pages 44-45, provides a look at the impact on the team of the four Interaction Styles of In-Charge, Chart-the-Course, Get-Things-Going, and Behind-the-Scenes as well s the Interaction Style dynamics of Directing versus Informing communications and Initiating versus Responding roles.

4. Mapping the Team Using Cognitive Dynamics, pages 46-47, provides a look at the impact on the team of preferences for the eight cognitive processes of extraverted Sensing, introverted Sensing, extraverted iNtuiting, introverted iNtuiting, extraverted Thinking, introverted Thinking, extraverted Feeling, and introverted Feeling.

First answer the Who Am I? Questions. Then as you get to know your teammates better, fill in the information about them.

Who Am I?

Reference your type profile as well as your past experiences and areas of expertise. Remember you bring more than your type to the team.

What talents and skills do I bring to this team?

What doubts do I bring to this team?

What roles am I most comfortable filling?

What are my strengths?

What are my blind spots?

What do I need from others on this team to function at my highest and best level?

Who Are You?

Reference what your teammates have shared about their type profiles as well as their past experiences and areas of expertise. Remember they bring more than their type to the team.

What talents and skills do my teammates bring to this team?

What doubts have they expressed about this team?

What roles are my teammates most comfortable filling?

What are my teammates' strengths?

What are my teammates' blind spots?

What do my teammates need from others on this team to function at their highest and best level?

Mapping the Team Using Type Preferences

The type table on the right was created by Isabel Myers to display the types together that have the most in common. It is organized around the two middle letters in the type code called "function pairs." These two letters refer to the preferred mode of perception and the preferred mode of judgment for that type pattern. Using Myers's interpretation of Jung's theories, the focus is on the columns of the type table. Many type practitioners group people by these function pairs in activities that highlight differences and points of conflict. Myers also wanted to put the two types that share a preference for the same dominant function in the same attitude next to each other. For example, ISTJ and ISFJ both have dominant introverted Sensing (Si) preferences and are side by side. Her system works if you think of the table as a cylinder that puts INTP and ISTP side by side and ENTJ and ESTJ side by side.

		SENSING		INTUITING	
		THINKING	FEELING	FEELING	THINKING
INTROVERSION	JUDGING	ISTJ	ISFJ	INFJ	INTJ
	PERCEIVING	ISTP	ISFP	INFP	INTP
EXTRAVERSION	PERCEIVING	ESTP	ESFP	ENFP	ENTP
	JUDGING	ESTJ	ESFJ	ENFJ	ENTJ

The left side of the table displays the types with a Sensing preference, and the right side displays those with a preference for iNtuiting (iNtuition). The top half consists of the eight types that are introverted and the bottom half those that are extraverted. The top and bottom rows are the types with a Judging preference, and the two middle rows are the types with a Perceiving preference for dealing with the outer world. The outside columns display the types with a Thinking preference, and the middle columns display those with a Feeling preference.

Aspects of the Types	Characteristics
Looking at Preferences	
Extraversion vs. Introversion E/I	Extraversion is being primarily oriented to and energized by the world outside oneself. Introversion is being primarily oriented to and energized by the world inside oneself.
Sensing vs. iNtuiting S/N	Sensing refers to tangible, experiential awareness. Intuiting refers to symbolic, conceptual awareness.
Thinking vs. Feeling T/F	Thinking judgments are based on criteria or principles. Feeling judgments are based on appropriateness or worth.
Judging vs. Perceiving J/P	A Judging preference indicates liking to live one's outer life with closure and structure using the preferred judging process of Thinking or Feeling. A Perceiving preference indicates liking to live one's outer life in a more emergent manner using the preferred perceiving process of Sensing or iNtuiting.
Looking at Function Pairs	The columns of the type table list the functional pairs. This tells us the kind of information (Sensing or iNtuiting) we pay attention to and the kind of decisions (Thinking or Feeling) we tend to make.
Sensing and Thinking ST	Attention to the tangible realities based on current and past experiences with a focus on "objective" facts, criteria, or principles. A just-the-facts approach.
Sensing and Feeling SF	Attention to the tangible realities based on current and past experiences with a focus on the people and the values involved. A sensitive-and-caring approach.
iNtuiting and Thinking NT	Attention to concepts, meanings, interrelationships, and probable or possible futures with a focus on the principles and criteria involved. An abstract, problem-solving approach.
iNtuiting and Feeling NF	Attention to concepts, meanings, interrelationships, and probable or possible futures with a focus on the people and values involved. A growth-and-development approach.

Option: Type Preferences

Team Dynamics Using Type Preferences

Full type, preferences, and preference pairs can inform us of a number of team dynamics. Since the majority often determines norms, we can predict the norms that are likely to emerge in a team. Once these norms are made explicit, the group can decide whether to follow them or to consciously allow for other norms to operate. To look at the makeup of your team and determine the likely natural norms as well as the strengths, blind spots, and primary approach to the work of the team, consider these questions:

- What full types are represented on the team? What does that tell you about what the team is likely to be interested in doing? What is the type of the team leader?

- What full types (if any) are in the majority? How will that influence the team?

- What preferences are represented? Count the number of each preference represented on the team. What does this mix tell you about what this team will focus on?

- What functional pairs are represented? What does this mix tell you about how the group might gather information and make decisions?

- What are the anticipated strengths of your team? Based on the types and preferences represented, what will this team naturally do well?

- What whole types and preferences are in the minority and thus likely to not be respected or acknowledged? Who is likely to feel the most frustrated?

- What are the likely blind spots or pitfalls of this team? What types are not represented and therefore talents missing from the team?

- Who on the team has experiences to help the team make up for the blind spots?

- What points of conflict might occur? How might the team be split or polarized?

- How is change likely to be dealt with by this team? Consider how each type present on the team deals with change.

Mapping the Team Using Temperament

As David Keirsey developed his theory of the four temperaments, he began to display them to show the aspects the four temperaments have in common. As Linda Berens expanded on his work, she began to consistently display the Catalyst™ (the types with N and F in their type codes) and the Stabilizer™ (those with S and J in their codes) on the top of the matrix to show that these two temperaments have in common a social attitude—they tend to take more affiliative roles and focus on interdependence. The Theorist™ temperament (with N and T in their codes) and the Improviser™ (with S and P in their codes) are on the bottom of the matrix to show that they have in common a more pragmatic, do-what-it-takes attitude that focuses on autonomy and independence. On the left are the two temperaments that tend to speak abstractly (Catalyst™ and Theorist™) and on the right are the two that tend to speak in more tangible terms (Stabilizer™ and Improviser™).

Since temperament theory is based in the Gestalt-Field-Systems school of thought, the focus is on thematic wholes rather than juxtaposition of traits. Here are some major themes of the four temperament patterns.

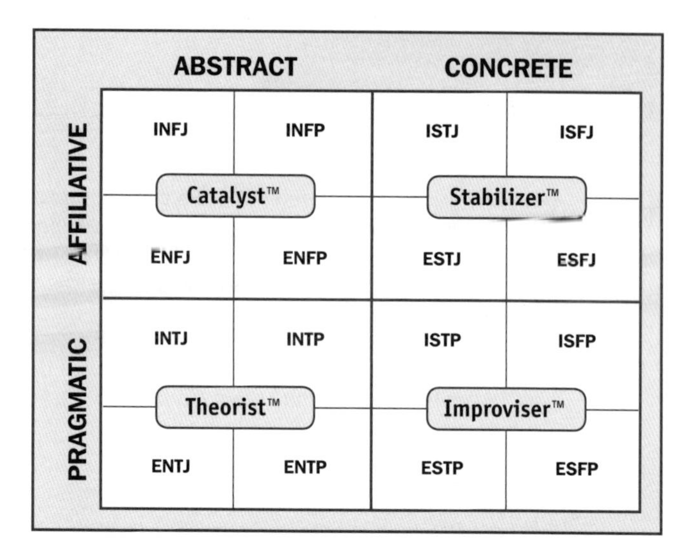

Each temperament has four variations. This gets us to sixteen type patterns, which behaviorally match the sixteen type patterns arrived at through Isabel Myers's interpretation of Jung. People who use temperament in their understanding of the types find the temperament matrix communicates a lot to them very quickly, and they can see how each type has something in common with every other type as well as how they are different.

	Improviser™	Stabilizer™	Theorist™	Catalyst™
Core Needs	• Freedom to act on needs of the moment • Having an impact	• Membership, belonging, a place • Responsibility	• Knowledge and competence • Mastery	• Deep meaning and significance • Unique identity
Some Core Values	• Variety • Skillful performance	• Security • Predictability	• Progress • Logical consistency	• Authenticity • Empathic relationships
Talent	• Tactics • Performance	• Logistics • Protecting	• Strategy • Design	• Diplomacy • Advocacy
Language	• Colloquial • Stories and anecdotes • Colorful	• Customary • Comparisons • Factual	• Precise • Conditionals • Scholarly	• Global • Metaphors • Dramatic
Time Sense	Present	Past	Timeless	Future
Type Code	_ S _ P	_ S _ J	_ NT _	_ NF _

Option: Temperament

Team Dynamics Using Temperament

Temperament can inform us of a number of team dynamics. Since norms are often determined by the majority, we can predict the norms that are likely to emerge in a team. Once these norms are made explicit, the group can decide whether to follow them or to consciously allow for other norms to operate. To look at the makeup of a team and determine the likely natural norms as well as the strengths, blind spots, and primary approach to the work of the team, consider these questions:

- What full types and temperaments are represented on the team? What does that tell you about what the team is likely to be interested in doing? What is the temperament of the team leader?
- What full types and temperaments (if any) are in the majority? How will that influence the team?
- What are the anticipated strengths of your team? Based on the full types and temperaments represented, what will this team naturally do well?
- What full types and temperaments are in the minority and thus likely to not be respected or acknowledged?
- What are the likely blind spots or pitfalls of this team? What full types and temperaments are not represented and therefore talents missing from the team? What value perspectives are not represented?
- Who on the team has experiences to help the team make up for the blind spots?
- What points of conflict might occur? Consider different value perspectives, time orientations, Abstract versus Concrete language, Affiliative versus Pragmatic roles.
- How is change likely to be dealt with by this team? Consider values and time orientation as well as each full type's response to change.

Mapping the Team Using Interaction Styles

The Interaction Styles model is based on observable behavior patterns of interaction with others, especially when we are trying to influence others. These patterns tell us the how of our behavior,

The Interaction Styles can be arranged in a matrix that describes their similarities and things in common. The left side of the matrix displays the types with a Directing communication style and a time and task focus. On the right side of the matrix are the types with an Informing communication style and a process and motivation focus. On the top of the matrix are the types who tend to take a Responding role with others, waiting to see what is happening before interacting. On the bottom of the matrix are the types who tend to take an Initiating role with others, making the first move. Diagonally, the types in the upper right-hand quadrant and the lower left-hand quadrant share an interest in control. The types in the upper left-hand quadrant and the lower right-hand quadrant share an interest in movement.

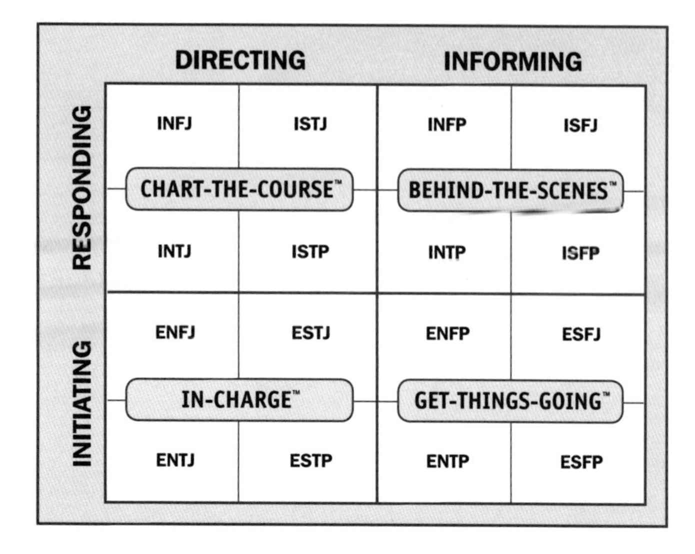

Each of the four Interaction Style patterns has four variations. This gets us to sixteen type patterns, which behaviorally match the sixteen type patterns arrived at through Isabel Myers's interpretation of Jung. People who use Interaction Styles in their understanding of the types find the Interaction Styles matrix communicates a lot to them very quickly, and they can see how each type has something in common with every other type as well as how they are different.

	In-Charge™	Chart-the-Course™	Get-Things-Going™	Behind-the-Scenes™
Core Drive	Urgent need to accomplish in a timely manner	Pressing need to anticipate and have points of reference	Urgent need to involve others and be involved	Pressing need to integrate and consider many sources
Aim	Get an achievable result	Get a desired result	Get an embraced result	Get the best result possible
Core Belief	It's worth the risk to go ahead and act or decide.	It's worth the effort and time to think ahead to reach the goal.	It's worth the energy to involve everyone and get everyone to want to...	It's worth the time to integrate and reconcile many inputs.
Some Talents	• Supervise • Mobilize resources • Mentor • Execute actions	• Devise a plan • Illuminate • Give guidance • Monitor progress	• Facilitate • Make things easy for others • Share insights • Explore options	• Support others • Define specifications • Clarify values and issues • Produce
Decision Making	Quick decisions	Deliberate decisions	Consensual decisions	Consultative decisions
Type Codes	ESTP, ESTJ, ENTJ, ENFJ	ISTP, ISTJ, INTJ, INFJ	ESFP, ESFJ, ENTP, ENFP	ISFP, ISFJ, INTP, INFP

Option: Interaction Styles

Team Dynamics Using the Interaction Styles Matrix

Interaction Styles can inform us of a number of team dynamics. Since norms are often determined by the majority, we can predict the norms that are likely to emerge in a team. Once these norms are made explicit, the group can decide whether to follow them or to consciously allow for other norms to operate. To look at the makeup of a team and determine the likely natural norms as well as the strengths, blind spots, and primary approach to the work of the team, consider these questions:

- What full types and Interaction Styles are represented on the team? What does that tell you about what the team is likely to be interested in doing? What is the Interaction Style of the team leader?

- What full types and Interaction Styles (if any) are in the majority? How will that influence the team?

- What are the anticipated strengths of your team? Based on the full types and Interaction Styles represented, what will this team naturally do well?

- What full types and Interaction Styles are in the minority and thus likely to not be respected or acknowledged?

- What are the likely blind spots or pitfalls of this team? What full types and Interaction Styles are not represented and therefore talents missing from the team? What value perspectives are not represented?

- Who on the team has experiences to help the team make up for the blind spots?

- What points of conflict might occur? Consider different drives, aims, core beliefs, Directing versus Informing, Initiating versus Responding.

- How is change likely to be dealt with by this team? Consider drives and aim as well as each full type's response to change.

Mapping the Team
Using Cognitive Dynamics

Carl Jung identified eight cognitive processes (also called functions or mental processes). Each type code stands for a pattern of these eight cognitive processes. John Beebe, a modern Jungian analyst, developed a model of each of the patterns in terms of the archetypal role each process plays in the pattern. The table below lists the sixteen type patterns and some user-friendly terms for the roles of each process in each pattern.

ROLES OF PROCESSES		Promoter Executor™ ESTP	Motivator Presenter™ ESFP	Planner Inspector™ ISTJ	Protector Supporter™ ISFJ	Explorer Inventor™ ENTP	Discoverer Advocate™ ENFP	Conceptualizer Director™ INTJ	Foreseer Developer™ INFJ	Implementor Supervisor™ ESTJ	Strategist Mobilizer™ ENTJ	Analyzer Operator™ ISTP	Designer Theorizer™ INTP	Facilitator Caretaker™ ESFJ	Envisioner Mentor™ ENFJ	Composer Producer™ ISFP	Harmonizer Clarifier™ INFP
+ Leading - Dominating	1st	S_e	S_e	S_i	S_i	N_e	N_e	N_i	N_i	T_e	T_e	T_i	T_i	F_e	F_e	F_i	F_i
+ Supporting - Overprotective	2nd	T_i	F_i	T_e	F_e	T_i	F_i	T_e	F_e	S_i	N_i	S_e	N_e	S_i	N_i	S_e	N_e
+ Relief - Unsettling	3rd	F_e	T_e	F_i	T_i	F_e	T_e	F_i	T_i	N_e	S_e	N_i	S_i	N_e	S_e	N_i	S_i
+ Aspirational™ - Projective	4th	N_i	N_i	N_e	N_e	S_i	S_i	S_e	S_e	F_i	F_i	F_e	F_e	T_i	T_i	T_e	T_e
- Opposing + Backup	5th	S_i	S_i	S_e	S_e	N_i	N_i	N_e	N_e	T_i	T_i	T_e	T_e	F_i	F_i	F_e	F_e
- Critical + Discovery	6th	T_e	F_e	T_i	F_i	T_e	F_e	T_i	F_i	S_e	N_e	S_i	N_i	S_e	N_e	S_i	N_i
- Deceiving + Comedic	7th	F_i	T_i	F_e	T_e	F_i	T_i	F_e	T_e	N_i	S_i	N_e	S_e	N_i	S_i	N_e	S_e
- Devilish + Transformative	8th	N_e	N_e	N_i	N_i	S_e	S_e	S_i	S_i	F_e	F_e	F_i	F_i	T_e	T_e	T_i	T_i

Se: Experiencing the immediate context; noticing changes and opportunities for action; being drawn to act on the physical world; accumulating experiences; scanning for visible reactions and relevant data; recognizing "what is."

Si: Reviewing past experiences; "what is" evoking "what was"; seeking detailed information and links to what is known; recalling stored impressions; accumulating data; recognizing the way things have always been.

Ne: Interpreting situations and relationships; picking up meanings and interconnections; being drawn to change "what is" for "what could possibly be"; noticing what is not said and threads of meaning emerging across multiple contexts.

Ni: Foreseeing implications and likely effects without external data; realizing "what will be"; conceptualizing new ways of seeing things; envisioning transformations; getting an image of profound meaning or far-reaching symbols.

Te: Ordering; segmenting; organizing for efficiency; systematizing; applying logic; structuring; checking for consequences; monitoring for standards or specifications being met; setting boundaries, guidelines, and parameters; deciding if something is working or not.

Ti: Analyzing; categorizing; evaluating according to principles and whether something fits the framework or model; figuring out the principles on which something works; checking for inconsistencies; clarifying definitions to get more precision.

Fe: Connecting; considering others and the group—organizing to meet their needs and honor their values and feelings; maintaining societal, organizational, or group values; adjusting and accommodating others; deciding if something is appropriate or acceptable to others.

Fi: Valuing; considering importance and worth; reviewing for incongruity; evaluating something based on the truths on which it is based; clarifying values to achieve accord; deciding if something is of significance and worth standing up for.

Option: Cognitive Dynamics

Team Dynamics Using the Cognitive Dynamics Model

Cognitive Dynamics can inform us of a number of team dynamics. Since the majority often determines norms, we can predict the norms that are likely to emerge in a team. Once these norms are made explicit, the group can decide whether to follow them or to consciously allow for other norms to operate. To look at the makeup of your team and determine the likely natural norms as well as the strengths, blind spots, and primary approach to the work of the team, consider these questions:

- What full types are represented on the team? What does that tell you about what the team is likely to be interested in doing? What is the type of the team leader?
- What full types (if any) are in the majority? How will that influence the team?
- What cognitive processes are represented as Leading (Dominant) or Supporting (Auxiliary)? Count the number of each preference represented on the team. What does this mix tell you about what this team will focus on?
- What are the anticipated strengths of your team? Based on the types and cognitive processes represented, what will this team naturally do well?
- What full types and cognitive processes are in the minority and thus likely to not be respected or acknowledged? Who is likely to feel the most frustrated?
- What are the likely blind spots or pitfalls of this team? What types and cognitive processes are not represented and therefore talents missing from the team? What information is likely to be missed? What kinds of decisions might be difficult and therefore avoided?
- Who on the team has experiences to help the team make up for the blind spots?
- What cognitive processes are in the Deceiving or Devilish roles and are therefore likely to be triggered in times of stress?
- What points of conflict might occur? How might team members trigger each other, such as when one team member's Leading role process (Dominant) is another's Devilish role process or when the same dominants compete?
- How is change likely to be dealt with by this team? Consider how each type present on the team deals with change.

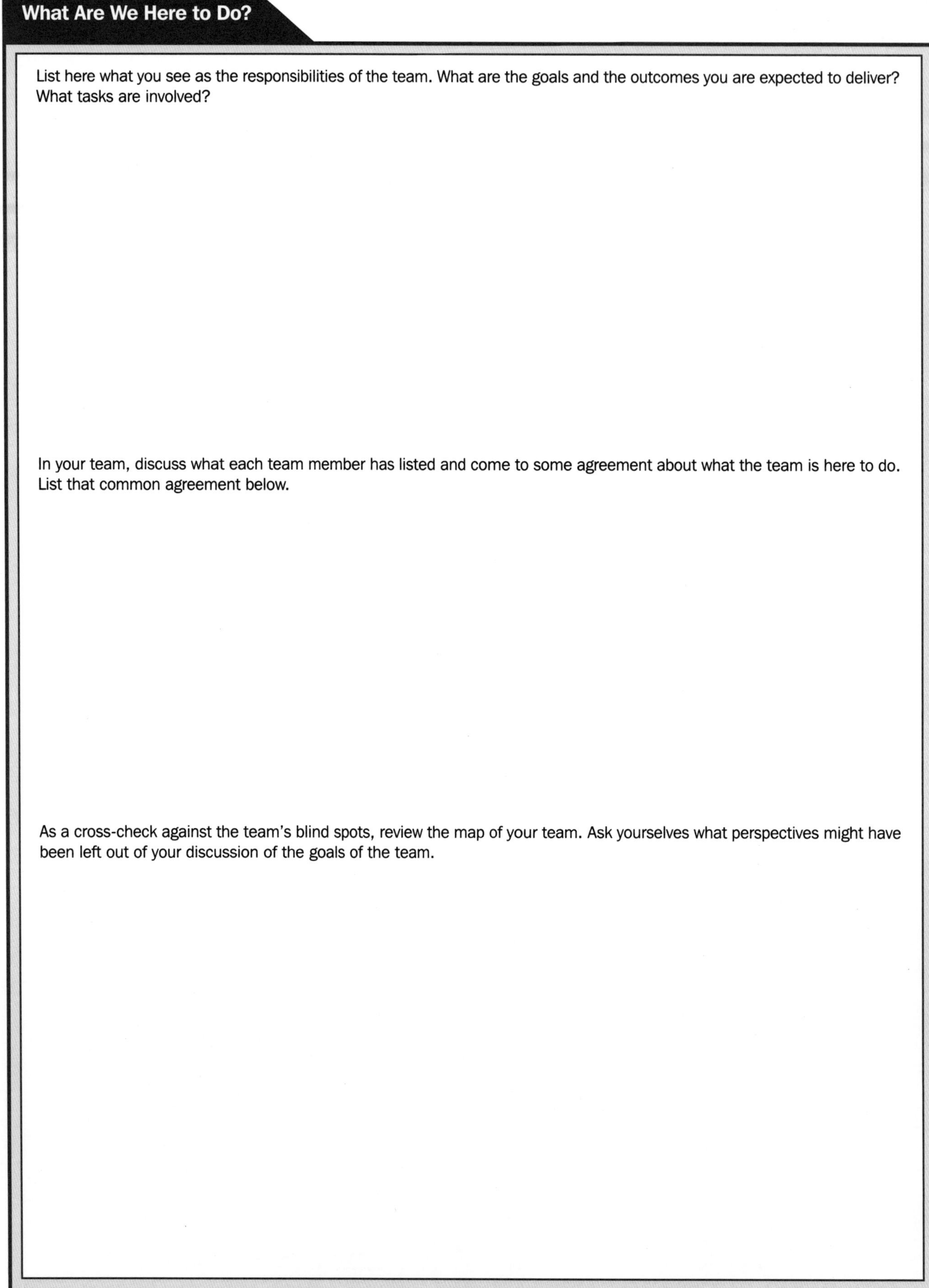

What Are We Here to Do?

List here what you see as the responsibilities of the team. What are the goals and the outcomes you are expected to deliver? What tasks are involved?

In your team, discuss what each team member has listed and come to some agreement about what the team is here to do. List that common agreement below.

As a cross-check against the team's blind spots, review the map of your team. Ask yourselves what perspectives might have been left out of your discussion of the goals of the team.

Process Norms

Group norms are sets of shared expectations and agreed-upon ground rules. Often these norms are unconscious and operate as the unwritten rules of the group. People know they exist only when a norm is violated and team members get upset or team functioning breaks down. Effective teams often take a more active role in surfacing these unwritten "rules" and actively establish the norms they want to follow. There are two kinds of norms—operational and process. In most work groups much attention is given to the operational norms, such as who's going to do what by when. However, having good process norms is what distinguishes a high performing team that maximizes diversity from a team that ignores diversity. When diversity is ignored, the output of the team suffers because contributions are missed and team members may withdraw their involvement. When diversity is ignored, energy may be wasted in needless conflict and resistance.

Have a discussion with your team members about the group norms the team will follow. Use the questions to guide you in agreeing on the process and operational norms you want to follow in your team.

REMEMBER: When this step is skipped, more wasteful conflict is likely to occur that will unnecessarily interfere with the work of the team. Facing conflicts during an active discussion of these issues will save much time and energy later.

Process Norms

Below are some examples of process norms for you to consider. Check off the ones the team agrees to try on. Edit them to fit your team.

- ❑ We will not ignore seriously intended contributions.
- ❑ We will check to make sure we know what a speaker means by a contribution before we agree or disagree with it.
- ❑ We recognize that each team member speaks only for himself or herself and will let others speak for themselves.
- ❑ All contributions will be viewed as belonging to the team to be used or not as the team decides.
- ❑ We will each participate but in different and complementary ways.
- ❑ Whenever the team senses it is having trouble getting work done, we will try to find out why.
- ❑ The team recognizes that whatever it does is what it has chosen to do. We recognize that an effective team makes decisions openly rather than by default.
- ❑ The team will bring conflict into the open and deal with it. We recognize that conflict is unavoidable. We will use what we know about the diversity on the team and deal openly with these conflicts in order to achieve a better outcome and more effective team functioning.
- ❑ The team believes behavior that hinders its work happens because the team allows or even wants it. Such behavior is not just the result of a "problem" team member.
- ❑ The team will give individuals opportunities to concentrate on issues that are important to them. We agree to help each individual work through an issue in his or her own preferred way rather than moving on or changing the subject.
- ❑ We agree to relate in a mutually constructive way, rather than in a competitive way.

Operational Norms

As a team, discuss and agree upon answers to the following operational issues:

- Who's going to do what?
- What are the processes we'll use to get the work done?
- How will we decide if we have to meet or if there are alternative ways of sharing information?
- When will we meet? How often? Where? How long?
- Who will convene our meetings?
- How will we communicate between meetings?
- How will we handle non-attendance at meetings? Turning in/reporting on assignments? Exchanging information? Obtaining meeting notes? Other?
- How will we get meetings started on time? How will we handle late arrivals?
- What roles will we need to operate effectively during our meetings? Who will take on each role?
- How will we go about generating ideas as a group? Brainstorming meetings? Round robin e-mails? Other?
- How will we capture suggestions and ideas? Charts? E-mails? Meeting minutes? Other?
- What ground rules do we need for our meetings? Do we want them posted?
- How will we handle not meeting commitments?
- What decision rule will we use to make our decisions? Consensus? Majority rules? Leader makes the decisions after consultation? Other?
- How are we going to honor different decision-making styles?
- How will we indicate our level of agreement with ideas and suggestions?
- How will we summarize decisions and actions at the end of a discussion or meeting?

Agreements

Agreements for Managing Team Dynamics

Now that you have looked at and discussed some process and operational norms in general, add in how you will take typological differences into account as you work together on your team.

Review the map of your team. What agreements will you make to

- Be sure you listen to each team member, including those in the minority?
- Cover the blind spots or pitfalls of the team? Who on the team has experience in the blind spot areas and can fill in? Who on the team will take responsibility for being sure that blind spot areas are represented in discussions and decisions?
- Maximize our varying talents for tactics, logistics, strategy, and diplomacy?
- Handle our different approaches to conflict?
- Pay attention to our different responses to change? And show respect for each other's needs when change is difficult?

How Are We Doing?

What evaluation measures will we seek for our processes working together as a team?

What evaluation measures will we seek for the desired outcomes of the team?

How often will we stop and check in to see how we are doing?

Who will be responsible for bringing the check-in process to the attention of the group?

Case Study: The Company Picnic

To give you an example of applying type knowledge to the working of a team, we have developed a case study that will be mapped according to the four different models.

The Company Picnic

The Nature of the Organization, the Team, and the Work

A task force has been formed and charged with planning the fourth annual company picnic, to be held in six months, for their small, entrepreneurial, family-run technology company. This is the first time this group of individuals has worked together on a project. Task force members were selected because they are seen as informal leaders in their areas. Lisa is the nominal leader of the team, since she works in Human Resources and has spearheaded this event since it started. Most of the company's seventy-seven staff members look forward to this now-annual event as a way to get to know the growing number of new staff members, celebrate their successes, and renew their commitment to one another and the company founder.

Who Am I? Who Are You?

- Lisa, ENFP, human resources analyst, formerly a conference planner
- Rob, ISFJ, technician, the founder's nephew
- Kathy, ESTJ, purchasing agent, new to the company—only four months on the job
- Juan, ISTP, project manager
- Sam, ESTP, design lead

Who Are We Together?

To look at the makeup of a team and determine the likely natural norms as well as the strengths, blind spots, and primary approach to the work of the team, consider the questions in Section 5, Applying the Five Essential Issues: Mapping the Team—Team Dynamics using the Type Preferences (page 40), Temperament (page 42), Interaction Styles (page 44), and Cognitive Dynamics (page 46). Analysis using each of these models follows.

What Are We Here to Do?

The task force's responsibilities include:

- Surveying employees to gather ideas and find out what people want to do
- Deciding the date, time, and schedule of the event
- Determining the location and handling arrangements
- Choosing and coordinating the activities
- Arranging for food and beverages
- Marketing/promoting the event
- Assuming responsibility for the budget and for negotiating any vendor contracts

Who Are We Together?

Type Preferences

		SENSING — THINKING	SENSING — FEELING	INTUITING — FEELING	INTUITING — THINKING
INTROVERSION	JUDGING	ISTJ	ISFJ ROB	INFJ	INTJ
INTROVERSION	PERCEIVING	ISTP JUAN	ISFP	INFP	INTP
EXTRAVERSION	PERCEIVING	ESTP SAM	ESFP	ENFP LISA	ENTP
EXTRAVERSION	JUDGING	ESTJ KATHY	ESFJ	ENFJ	ENTJ

Remember: Individuals of different personality types may shift to take the roles needed by the mission of the team and thus may look like other types.

Team Dynamics Using Type Preferences

Full type, preferences, and preference pairs can inform us of a number of team dynamics. Since the majority often determines norms, we can predict the norms that are likely to emerge in a team. Once these norms are made explicit, the group can decide whether to follow them or to consciously allow for other norms to operate. To look at the makeup of your team and determine the likely natural norms as well as the strengths, blind spots, and primary approach to the work of the team, consider these questions:

Type Preferences

What full types are represented on the team? What does that tell you about what the team is likely to be interested in doing? What is the type of the team leader?

Lisa—ENFP: Discoverer Advocate™—will probably want to engage others and seek consensual decisions. As the leader, Lisa may play a catalytic role through her enthusiasm for what the picnic will do for morale and community.

Rob—ISFJ: Protector Supporter™—will probably be interested in serving the needs of the individuals in the company and will focus on making sure everything is taken care of. As a family member, he may bring a sense of tradition and concern for protecting the resources as well as the people in the company.

Kathy—ESTJ: Implementor Supervisor™—will probably focus on organizing the event efficiently and within budget. Since she is fairly new to the organization she may want to know what has been done before.

Juan—ISTP: Analyzer Operator™—will probably approach the task as a problem to be solved and then focus on crafting a clever solution to whatever problems come up.

Sam—ESTP: Promoter Executor™—will probably be interested in making things happen, thriving on action and freedom to use all resources.

What full types (if any) are in the majority? How will that influence the team?

No full types are in the majority, but Juan, ISTP, and Sam, ESTP, have a lot in common and so there will likely be a lot of focus on getting the facts and then acting on them rather than discussing lots of ideas.

What preferences are represented? Count the number of each preference represented on the team. What does this mix tell you about what this team will focus on?

More team members have Extraverted Preferences than Introverted Preferences, so there is likely to be pressure for immediate discussion and talking about things rather than giving people time to go away and reflect and then discuss.

More team members have Thinking preferences than Feeling preferences, so the team will probably focus more on data than on the people issues, although the nature of their task may cause each of them to use the Feeling process when deciding about what will please people at the picnic.

More team members have Sensing preferences than iNtuiting preferences, so the team will probably want the tangible details ironed out and might ignore the more subtle meanings brought in by the lone person with an iNtuiting preference.

More team members have Perceiving preferences than Judging preferences, so their process is likely to be more emergent and open-ended.

What functional pairs are represented? What does this mix tell you about how the group might gather information and make decisions?

ST, SF, and NF are represented; NT is missing. This might mean a focus on practical problem solving yet with concern for the people issues.

What are the anticipated strengths of your team? Based on the types and preferences represented, what will this team naturally do well?

Anticipated strengths are in representation of all the preferences. This team will naturally attend to the facts and details of getting this picnic planned and organized. If everyone is listened to, a balance of attention will be given to the people issues and the opeTheorist™ issues.

What whole types and preferences are in the minority and thus likely to not be respected or acknowledged? Who is likely to feel the most frustrated?

Lisa is likely to feel the most frustrated, as she is the most in the minority.

What are the likely blind spots or pitfalls of this team? What types are not represented and therefore talents missing from the team?

Missing the functional pair of NT, this team might miss out on thinking of less obvious contingencies and might miss marketing opportunities.

What points of conflict might occur? How might the team be split or polarized?

This team might be polarized around people issues and task issues.

Who Are We Together? Temperament

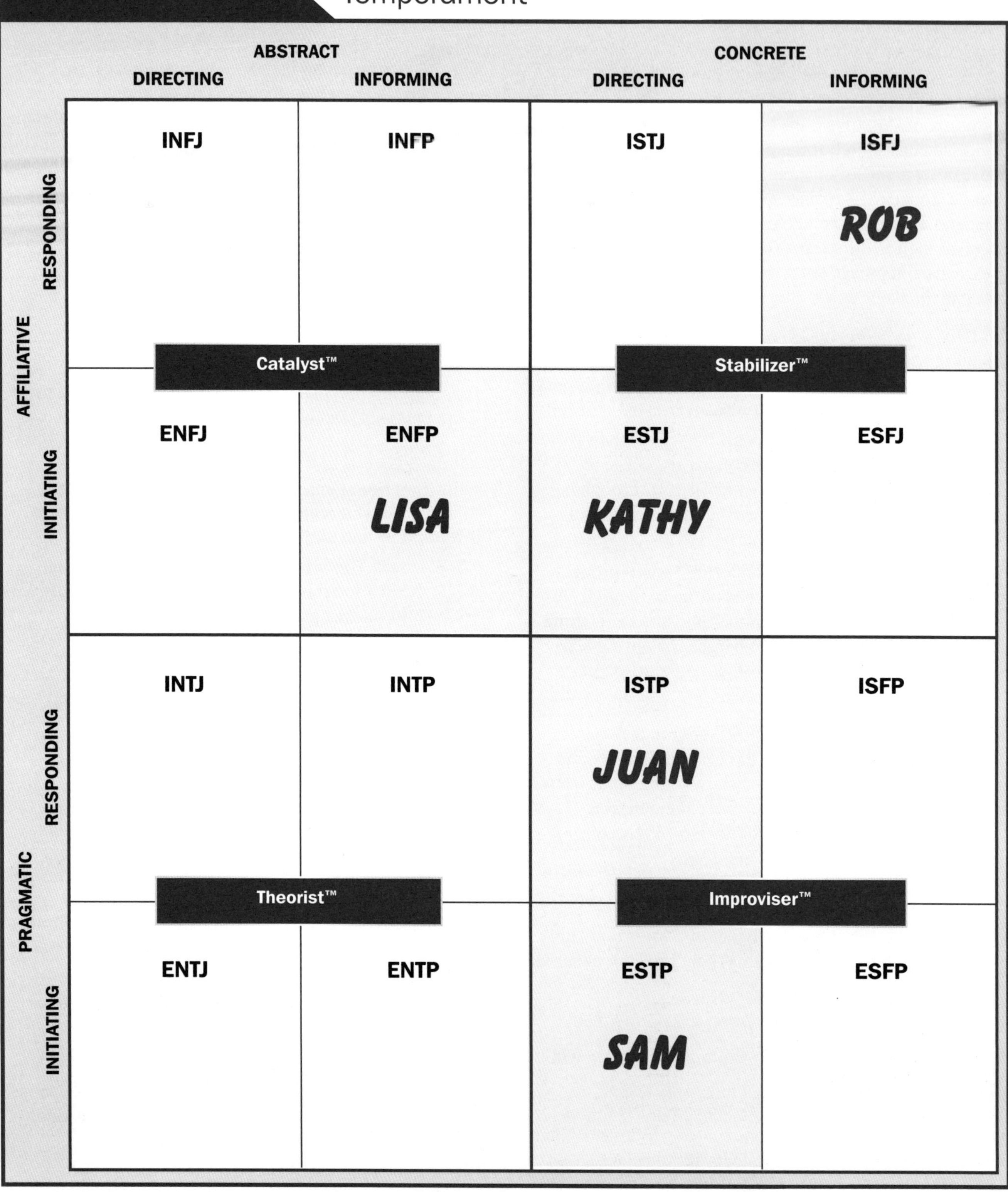

Remember: Individuals of different personality types may shift to take the roles needed by the mission of the team and thus may look like other temperaments.

Team Dynamics Using Temperament

Temperament can inform us of a number of team dynamics. Since norms are often determined by the majority, we can predict the norms that are likely to emerge in a team. Once these norms are made explicit, the group can decide whether to follow them or to consciously allow for other norms to operate. To look at the makeup of a team and determine the likely natural norms as well as the strengths, blind spots, and primary approach to the work of the team, consider these questions:

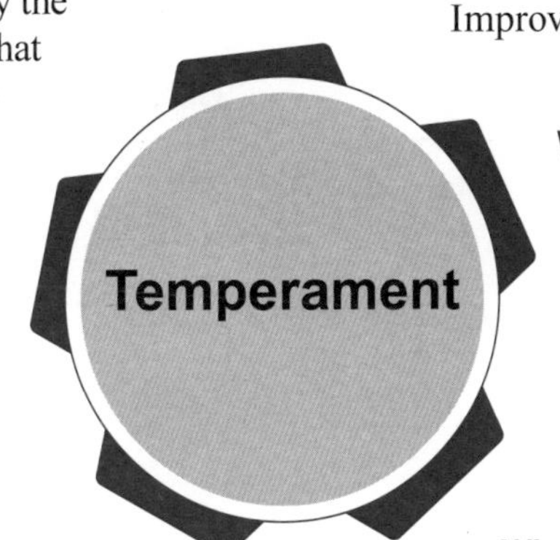

What full types and temperaments are represented on the team? What does that tell you about what the team is likely to be interested in doing? What is the temperament of the team leader?

Lisa—ENFP: Discoverer Advocate™—will likely want to engage others and seek consensual decisions. As a Catalyst™, Lisa will likely bring a talent for diplomacy to the team. As the leader, she will likely play a catalytic role through her enthusiasm for what the picnic will do for morale and community.

Rob—ISFJ: Protector Supporter™—will likely be interested in serving the needs of the individuals in the company and will focus on making sure everything is taken care of. As a Stabilizer™, Rob will probably bring a talent for logistics to the team. As a family member, he may bring a sense of tradition and concern for protecting the resources as well as the people in the company.

Kathy—ESTJ: Implementor Supervisor™—will likely focus on organizing the event efficiently and within budget. As a Stabilizer™, Kathy will probably bring a talent for logistics to the team. Since she is fairly new to the organization she may want to know what has been done before.

Juan—ISTP: Analyzer Operator™—will likely approach the task as a problem to be solved and then focus on crafting a clever solution to whatever problems come up. As an Improviser™, Juan will probably bring a talent for tactics to the team.

Sam—ESTP: Promoter Executor™—will likely be interested in making things happen, thriving on action and freedom to use all resources. As an Improviser™, Sam will probably bring a talent for tactics to the team.

What full types and temperaments (if any) are in the majority? How will that influence the team?

Stabilizers™ and Improvisers™ are evenly split, so there is probably not going to be a heavy influence of one temperament over another unless power differences come into play. There is more likely going to be a focus on Concrete communications since Stabilizers™ and Improvisers™ share that dimension of temperament.

What are the anticipated strengths of your team? Based on the full types and temperaments represented, what will this team naturally do well?

A strength is having some diversity. The team will likely attend to the details of getting the picnic planned and make sure it is fun for all.

What full types and temperaments are in the minority and thus likely to not be respected or acknowledged?

ENFP and Catalyst™ are in the minority and so might have a hard time getting ideas listened to. The difference here is that Lisa has position power and has planned this event before. Her prior experience would be important for both the Stabilizers™ and the Improvisers™ and so they might listen to her more.

What are the likely blind spots or pitfalls of this team? What full types and temperaments are not represented and therefore talents missing from the team? What value perspectives are not represented?

The likely blind spot is the absence of the talents and perspectives of the Theorist™ temperament, so the team might be missing a truly strategic focus and a value on theoretical accuracy and thinking of all the influencing factors. However, that may not be extremely important for the task of the team since long-range strategy would not be so relevant.

What points of conflict might occur? Consider different value perspectives, time orientations, Abstract versus Concrete language, Affiliative versus Pragmatic roles.

Conflict might occur between the Stabilizer™ value on conserving resources and the Improviser™ value on expedient action and also between an Affiliative versus Pragmatic approach to roles. The Stabilizers™ will likely want to adhere to traditions, and the Improvisers™ might want to do something different than what was done before. The lone Catalyst™ might feel stuck in the middle.

How is change likely to be dealt with by this team? Consider values and time orientation as well as each full type's response to change.

This team might resist change at first. Lisa, as a Catalyst™, will likely want to have consensus and want to spend time bridging differences, while the two Improvisers™ will want to just get to it and not discuss it much. The Stabilizers™ may want to weigh things according to how they were done before and especially consider the economics of it all.

Interaction Styles

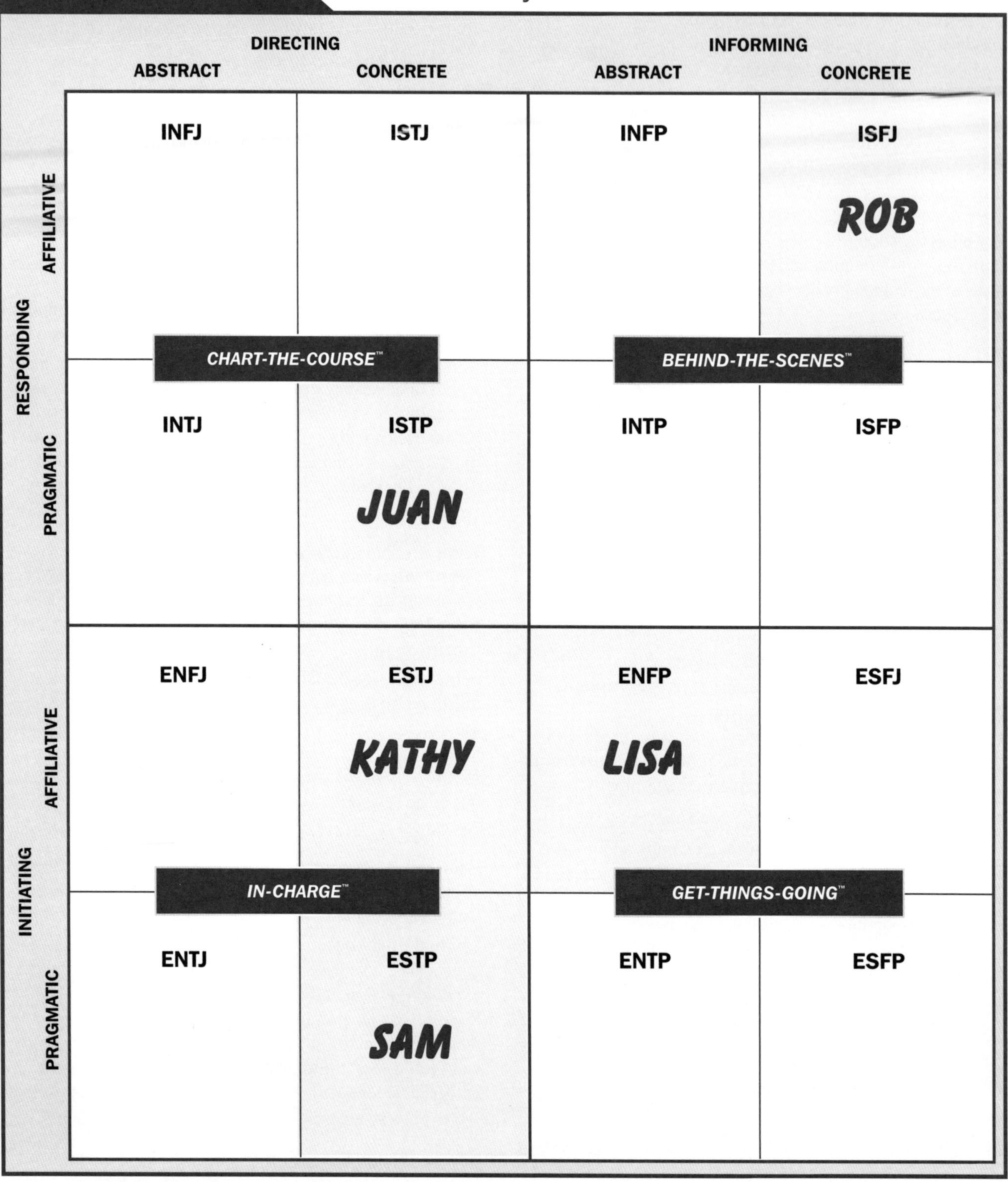

Remember: Individuals of different personality types may shift to take the roles needed by the mission of the team and thus may look like other interaction styles.

Team Dynamics Using Interaction Styles

Interaction Styles can inform us of a number of team dynamics. Since norms are often determined by the majority, we can predict the norms that are likely to emerge in a team. Once these norms are made explicit, the group can decide whether to follow them or to consciously allow for other norms to operate. To look at the makeup of a team and determine the likely natural norms as well as the strengths, blind spots, and primary approach to the work of the team, consider these questions:

Interaction Styles

What full types and Interaction Styles are represented on the team? What does that tell you about what the team is likely to be interested in doing? What is the Interaction Style of the team leader?

Lisa—ENFP: Discoverer Advocate™—will probably want to engage others and seek consensual decisions. As the leader, she may play a catalytic role through her enthusiasm for what the picnic will do for morale and community. Lisa's Interaction Style is Get-Things-Going, and she is likely to get things off to an energetic start and work hard to keep everyone involved.

Rob—ISFJ: Protector Supporter™—will probably be interested in serving the needs of the individuals in the company and may focus on making sure everything is taken care of. As a family member, he will likely bring a sense of tradition and concern for protecting the resources as well as the people in the company. Rob's Behind-the-Scenes Interaction Style may play out as providing support to get the best possible result.

Kathy—ESTJ: Implementor Supervisor™—will probably focus on organizing the event efficiently and within budget. Since she is fairly new to the organization, she might want to know what has been done before. Kathy's Interaction Style is In-Charge, and she brings a focus on accomplishment and achievable results.

Juan—ISTP: Analyzer Operator™—will probably approach the task as a problem to be solved and then focus on crafting a clever solution to whatever problems come up. Juan's Chart-the-Course Interaction Style will likely lead him to want a plan of action with some way of checking progress along the way.

Sam—ESTP: Promoter Executor™—will probably be interested in making things happen, thriving on action and freedom to use all resources. Sam's Interaction Style is In-Charge, and he brings a focus on accomplishment and achievable results.

What full types and Interaction Styles (if any) are in the majority? How will that influence the team?

With two In-Charge styles, there may be a push for achievable results and quick decisions. They will want to control the resources and remove any obstacles to accomplishment.

What are the anticipated strengths of your team? Based on the full types and Interaction Styles represented, what will this team naturally do well?

A strength of this team is the balance of Interaction Styles as all are represented.

What full types and Interaction Styles are in the minority and thus likely to not be respected or acknowledged?

No real minority voice exists as to Interaction Styles. However, the quieter Responding styles, Rob (ISFJ) and Juan (ISTP), might have some trouble getting the chance they need to fully participate.

What are the likely blind spots or pitfalls of this team? What full types and Interaction Styles are not represented and therefore talents missing from the team? What drives are not represented?

None are missing, so the talents of each style can be brought to the task of the team.

What points of conflict might occur? Consider different decision-making styles, different aims, interest in Control versus interest in Movement, Directing versus Informing communication preferences, Initiating versus Responding role-taking styles.

Conflicts of pacing may occur between the faster paced Initiating and the slower paced Responding styles. Conflicts between Directing and Informing communication styles may lead to some confusion and discounting of others. There might be a push-pull between the two team members who have an In-Charge style if they don't feel that matters are under control.

How is change likely to be dealt with by this team? Consider control versus movement and different drives as well as each full type's response to change.

The Behind-the-Scenes style might want to make some changes in order to get a better result. The Get-Things-Going style might be prone to promote a change to increase the energy and involvement. Juan, as a Chart-the-Course style, will want to have time to analyze and determine the need for the change. The In-Charge styles will likely want to be sure everything is under control with the change.

Who Are We Together?

Cognitive Dynamics

	Promoter Executor™ ESTP **SAM**	Motivator Presenter™ ESFP	Explorer Inventor™ ENTP	Discoverer Advocate™ ENFP **LISA**	Implementor Supervisor™ ESTJ **KATHY**	Strategist Mobilizer™ ENTJ	Facilitator Caretaker™ ESFJ	Envisioner Mentor™ ENFJ
+ Leading - Dominating 1st	S_e	S_e	N_e	N_e	T_e	T_e	F_e	F_e
+ Supporting - Overprotective 2nd	T_i	F_i	T_i	F_i	S_i	N_i	S_i	N_i
+ Relief - Unsettling 3rd	F_e	T_e	F_e	T_e	N_e	S_e	N_e	S_e
+ AspiTheorist™ - Projective 4th	N_i	N_i	S_i	S_i	F_i	F_i	T_i	T_i
- Opposing + Backup 5th	S_i	S_i	N_i	N_i	T_i	T_i	F_i	F_i
- Critical + Discovery 6th	T_e	F_e	T_e	F_e	S_e	N_e	S_e	N_e
- Deceiving + Comedic 7th	F_i	T_i	F_i	T_i	N_i	S_i	N_i	S_i
- Devilish + Transformative 8th	N_e	N_e	S_e	S_e	F_e	F_e	T_e	T_e

	Planner Inspector™ ISTJ	Protector Supporter™ ISFJ **ROB**	Conceptualizer Director™ INTJ	Foreseer Developer™ INFJ	Analyzer Operator™ ISTP **JUAN**	Designer Theorizer™ INTP	Composer Producer™ ISFP	Harmonizer Clarifier™ INFP
+ Leading - Dominating 1st	S_i	S_i	N_i	N_i	T_i	T_i	F_i	F_i
+ Supporting - Overprotective 2nd	T_e	F_e	T_e	F_e	S_e	N_e	S_e	N_e
+ Relief - Unsettling 3rd	F_i	T_i	F_i	T_i	N_i	S_i	N_i	S_i
+ AspiTheorist™ - Projective 4th	N_e	N_e	S_e	S_e	F_e	F_e	T_e	T_e
- Opposing + Backup 5th	S_e	S_e	N_e	N_e	T_e	T_e	F_e	F_e
- Critical + Discovery 6th	T_i	F_i	T_i	F_i	S_i	N_i	S_i	N_i
- Deceiving + Comedic 7th	F_e	T_e	F_e	T_e	N_e	S_e	N_e	S_e
- Devilish + Transformative 8th	N_i	N_i	S_i	S_i	F_i	F_i	T_i	T_i

Remember: Individuals of different personality types may shift to take the roles needed by the mission of the team and thus may look like other types.

Team Dynamics Using Cognitive Dynamics

Cognitive Dynamics can inform us of a number of team dynamics. Since the majority often determines norms, we can predict the norms that are likely to emerge in a team. Once these norms are made explicit, the group can decide whether to follow them or to consciously allow for other norms to operate. To look at the makeup of your team and determine the likely natural norms as well as the strengths, blind spots, and primary approach to the work of the team, consider these questions:

Cognitive Dynamics

What full types and preferred cognitive processes are represented on the team? What does that tell you about what the team is likely to be interested in doing? What are the preferred cognitive processes of the team leader?

Lisa—ENFP: Discover Advocate™—will probably engage frequently in interpreting the meanings behind different communications on the team. She is likely to focus on what could possibly be and enjoy brainstorming new ideas for the picnic project and come up with ways to change from what they did before. She will likely focus on the worth of different ideas and clarify values to achieve consensus.

Rob—ISFJ: Protector Supporter™—will probably focus first on what the picnic was like in the past and assume it will be the same this year. He will want to pay attention to all the details that need to be considered in light of what is good for the group and what will make others comfortable and at ease.

Kathy—ESTJ: Implementor Supervisor™—will probably focus on the order and sequence of what will happen, making sure the standards are set. She will also want to know what happen in the past.

Juan—ISTP: Analyzer Operator™—will probably approach the task first through analysis of the situation. Once it is figured out, then he'll want to act on solving whatever problems are seen.

Sam—ESTP: Promoter Executor™—will probably be noticing the reactions of team members and keying in to data that is relevant to the task. His focus will be on what the experience of the picnic will be like. He will likely do a quick analysis of any problems and be ready to instantly troubleshoot.

What full types (if any) are in the majority? How will that influence the team?

None are in the majority.

What cognitive processes are represented as Leading (dominant) or Supporting (auxiliary)? Count the number of each preference represented on the team. What does this mix tell you about what this team will focus on?

Two with Ti: Analyzing according to principles
Two with Si: Reviewing and recalling from the past
Two with Se: Experiencing and acting on what is actually there now
One with Ne: Intrepreting and inferring meanings
One with Te: Ordering and organizing according to criteria
One with Fe: Connecting with and considering others
One with Fi: Valuing and considering what is important

This team will probably focus on the past and the present but not too much on the future. Each decision-making process has enough representation that both people issues and task issues will be considered. The nature of the task—planning an event that will please people and needing to foresee their reactions—might activate Fe and Ni processes for each task force member.

What are the anticipated strengths of your team? Based on the types and cognitive processes represented, what will this team naturally do well?

This team's strength is in the representation of seven of the processes, so there will be a focus on most aspects of the situation requiring the use of the cognitive processes, except for Ni, Foreseeing implications.

What full types and cognitive processes are in the minority and thus likely to not be respected or acknowledged? Who is likely to feel the most frustrated?

Ne, interpreting, is in the minority so the team may have difficulty seeing and paying attention to a variety of ideas and possibilities. Lisa may become frustrated when the others on the team don't see the possibilities she sees.

What are the likely blind spots or pitfalls of this team? What types and cognitive processes are not represented and therefore talents missing from the team? What information is likely to be missed? What kinds of decisions might be difficult and therefore avoided?

The blind spot is likely to be lack of foresight (Ni, Foreseeing implications) as to how people will respond or the implications of this event for the larger picture of the organization.

What cognitive processes are in the Inferior or Devilish roles and are therefore likely to be triggered in times of stress?

A probable problem on this team is that Ne and Ni (the minority voice and the blind spot) are in the Aspirational role (inferior) or the shadow role positions for the majority of the team. In times of a lot of stress, these processes are likely to take on the negative side of the process and misinterpretations (lower level Ne) or overly pessimistic predictions (lower level Ni) might be activated so the more positive aspects of Ne and Ni would be blocked or ignored.

What points of conflict might occur? How might team members trigger each other, such as when one team member's dominant (or Leading role process) is another's Devilish role process or when the same dominants compete?

As stated above, Ne is Leading (dominant) for the nominal leader and it is Devilish for one team member and Aspirational (inferior) for another, so considerable conflict could occur about ideas and the possibilities of what to plan. Unexpressed dueling inferences may seed conflict over time.

How is change likely to be dealt with by this team? Consider how each type present on the team deals with change.

Given the minority voice of Ne and a blind spot of Ni, some changes might be seen as not even worth considering. With Si as one of the majority voices, there is likely to be a preference for keeping things the same—in the name of maintaining what was effective before.

Notepad

References

A

Berens, Linda V. *Dynamics of Personality Type: Understanding and Applying Jung's Cognitive Processes*. Huntington Beach, Calif.: Telos Publications, 2000.

Berens, Linda V. *Understanding Yourself and Others®: An Introduction to Interaction Styles 2.0*. Huntington Beach, Calif.: Telos Publications, 2007.

Berens, Linda V. *Understanding Yourself and Others®: An Introduction to the 4 Temperaments 3.0*. Huntington Beach, Calif.: Telos Publications, 2006.

Berens, Linda V., and Dario Nardi. *The 16 Personality Types: Descriptions for Self-Discovery*. Huntington Beach, Calif.: Telos Publications, 1999.

Berens, Linda V., et. al. *Quick Guide to the 16 Personality Types in Organizations: Understanding Personality Differences in the Workplace*. Huntington Beach, Calif.: Telos Publications, 2001.

Berens, Linda V., and Dario Nardi. *Understanding Yourself and Others®: An Introduction to the Personality Type Code*. Huntington Beach, Calif.: Telos Publications, 2004.

Cooper, Brad. *Quick Guide to the Four Temperaments and Sales: An Introduction to the Groundbreaking Sales® Methods*. Huntington Beach, Calif.: Telos Publications, 2003.

Cooper, Brad. and Linda V. Berens. *Groundbreaking Sales® Skills: Portable Sales Techniques™ to Ensure Success*. Huntington Beach, Calif.: Telos Publications, 2004.

Delunas, Eve, *Survival Games Personalities Play*. Carmel, Calif.: Sunflower Ink, 1992.

Dossett, Mary. and Julia Mallory. *Results by Design: Survival Skills for Project Managers*. Huntington Beach, Calif.: Telos Publications, 2004.

Dunning, Donna. *What's Your Type of Career?: Unlock the Secrets of Your Personality to Find Your Perfect Career Path*. Palo Alto, Calif.: Davies-Black Publishing, 2001.

Dunning, Donna. *Quick Guide to the Four Temperaments and Learning: Practical Tools and Strategies for Enhancing Learning Effectiveness*. Huntington Beach, Calif.: Telos Publications, 2003.

Dunning, Donna. *Quick Guide to the Four Temperaments and Change: Strategies for Navigating Workplace Change*. Huntington Beach, Calif.: Telos Publications, 2004.

Dunning, Donna. *TLC at Work*, Palo Alto, Calif.: Davies-Black Publishing, 2004.

Fairhurst, Alice M., and Lisa L. Fairhurst. *Effective Teaching, Effective Learning*. Palo Alto, Calif.: Consulting Psychologists Press, Inc., 1995.

Isachsen, Olaf, and Linda V. Berens. *Working Together: A Personality Centered Approach to Management*, 3d ed. San Juan Capistrano, Calif.: Institute for Management Development, 1995.

Gerke, Susan K., and Linda V. Berens *Quick Guide to Interaction Styles and Working Remotely: Strategies for Leading and Working in Virtual Teams*. Huntington Beach, Calif.: Telos Publications, 2003.

Gerke, Susan K., and Linda V. Berens The I in TEAM: *Accelerating Performance in Remote and Co-located Teams*. Huntington Beach, Calif.: Telos Publications, 2005.

Katzenbach, Jon R., and Douglas K. Smith. *The Wisdom of Teams*. New York: HarperCollins, 1999.

Keirsey, David, and Marilyn Bates, *Please Understand Me*. 3d ed. Del Mar, Calif.: Prometheus Nemesis Books, 1978.

Martin, Charles R. *Quick Guide to the 16 Personality Types and Career Mastery: Living with Purpose and Working Effectively*. Huntington Beach, Calif.: Telos Publications, 2003.

Michel, Sarah. *Perfecting Connecting®: Learning to Speak the Language of Others*. Audio. Huntington Beach, Calif.: Telos Publications, 2003.

Michel, Sarah. *Perfecting Connecting®: A Personal Guide to Mastering Networking in the Workplace*. Huntington Beach, Calif.: Telos Publications, 2004.

Myers, Isabel, and Peter Myers, contributor. *Gifts Differing*. Palo Alto, Calif.: Consulting Psychologists Press, 1995.

Nardi, Dario. *Character and Personality Type: Discovering Your Uniqueness for Career and Relationship Success*. Huntington Beach, Calif.: Telos Publications, 1999.

Nardi, Dario. *Multiple Intelligences and Personality Type: Tools and Strategies for Developing Human Potential*. Huntington Beach, Calif.: Telos Publications, 2000.

Nash, Susan. *Turning Team Performance Inside Out*. Palo Alto, Calif.: Davies-Black Publishing, 2000.

Pearman, Roger R. *Hard Wired Leadership: Unleashing the Power of Personality to Become a New Millennium Leader*. Palo Alto, Calif.: Davies-Black Publishing, 1997.

Pearman, Roger R. *Enhancing Leadership Effectiveness through Psychological Type*. Gainsville, Fla: Center for Applications of Psychological Type, 1999.

Segal, Marci. *Creativity and Personality Type: Tools for Understanding and Inspiring the Many Voices of Creativity*. Huntington Beach, Calif.: Telos Publications, 2001.

Segal, Marci. *Quick Guide to the Four Temperaments and Creativity: A Psychological Understanding of Innovation*. Huntington Beach, Calif.: Telos Publications, 2003.

Specht, David. *Lessons from the Window Seat: Achieving Shared Vision in the Workplace*. Huntington Beach, Calif.: Telos Publications, 2000.

On the Internet

16types.com: www.16types.com
4temperaments.com: www.4temperaments.com
BestFitType: www.bestfittype.com
Cognitive Processes: www.cognitiveprocesses.com
Interaction Styles: www.interactionstyles.com
Interstrength™ Associates: www.interstrength.com
Telos Publications: www.telospublications.com